Walking the Kiso Road

Walking the Kiso Road

A MODERN-DAY EXPLORATION OF OLD JAPAN

William Scott Wilson

Shambhala
BOULDER | 2015

Shambhala Publications, Inc.
4720 Walnut Street
Boulder, Colorado 80301
www.shambhala.com

9 8 7 6 5 4 3 2

Printed in The United States of America

⊗ This edition is printed on acid-free paper that meets the
American National Standards Institute z39.48 Standard.

♻ This book is printed on 30% postconsumer recycled paper.
For more information please visit www.shambhala.com.

Distributed in the United States by Penguin Random House
LLC and in Canada by Random House of Canada Ltd

Designed by Michael Russem

LIBRARY OF CONGRESS CATALOGING-IN-PUBLICATION DATA
Wilson, William Scott, 1944–
Walking the Kiso Road: a modern-day exploration of old Japan / William
Scott Wilson.
pages   cm
Includes bibliographical references.
ISBN 978-1-61180-125-5 (paperback)
1. Nakasendo (Japan)—Description and travel. 2. Wilson, William Scott,
1944– —Travel—Japan—Nakasendo. 3. Nakasendo (Japan)—History.
4. Nakasendo (Japan)—Social life and customs. I. Title.
DS894.59.N362W45 2015
952—dc23
2015000280

For my son, Henry Clay Wilson

Contents

Preface

Broadly speaking, there are two kinds of map: the grid and the story. The grid map places an abstract geometric meshwork upon a space, within which any item or individual can be coordinated. . . . The power of grid maps is that they make it possible for any individual or object to be located within an abstract totality of space. But their virtue is also their danger: that they reduce the world only to data, that they record space independent of being. Story maps, by contrast, represent a place as it is perceived by an individual or by a culture. They are records of specific journeys, rather than describing place within which innumerable journeys might take place. They are organized around the passage of the traveler, and their perimeters are the perimeters of the sight or experience of the traveler. Event and place are not fully distinguished, for they are often of the same substance.

—Robert Macfarlane, *The Wild Places*

A NUMBER OF YEARS AGO, I found myself seated comfortably on an early-morning local train heading out of the city of Nagoya. The train made a number of stops inside the city and then eventually moved on to the outskirts, passed the huge Oji Paper Company surrounded by its medieval-type walls, continued on with a stop now and then through farming communities with their rice and vegetable fields, and finally entered the low mountains bordering the broad, flat Nobi Plain. We paused briefly once or twice more to let people on or off at little unmanned stations and then moved on. It was early autumn, and the mountains were still predominantly green, but with some patches of fall colors and a persimmon tree covered with bright orange fruit here and there. Mists still hung in the folds of the low hills.

Finally, the train pulled into my stop, the village of Nagiso, tucked in almost like a narrow, quiet stream running through the valley, where I was informed that the minibus to my destination, Tsumago, would be leaving in two minutes. Grabbing my pack, I hurried out of the station and into a small parking lot where I purchased my ticket and got on board. Seconds later, we pulled out of the tiny village, moved out onto National Highway 17 (two lanes) and, following the Kiso River, drove through a hamlet or two and passed a large statuary company displaying granite grave markers and statues in various sizes of Buddhist saints, mysterious foxes, and some very large toads. Then, in less than fifteen minutes, we pulled into another small, open parking lot, where most of us got off.

There was nothing in particular to suggest that we had arrived at a very interesting place, but walking up through a narrow cobblestoned alleyway, I suddenly entered a village that had not changed much for two or three hundred years. Passed by the new (early twentieth century) railroad, it had "missed" the modernization that had brought other locales in the Kiso Valley almost up to date. The only street in town, the old Kiso Road, was extremely narrow and lined by shops, inns, and tiny restaurants where one could get not much more than a bowl of buckwheat noodles to eat—all made of weathered but well-kept wood and clearly of some age. I had stepped, with my nice nylon rucksack and Gortex raincoat, back in time.

A friendly shopkeeper pointed out the inn, the Matsushiro-ya, where I had booked two nights' lodging—again, an entirely wooden two-story structure with large wood-slatted sliding paper doors and floor-to-ceiling open sliding windows that took up the entire front of the edifice. As I signed the register, the proprietor—a short, fiftyish man with short cropped hair—informed me that the inn was some three hundred fifty years old and that he was the eighteenth generation of innkeeper there. Everything in the Matsushiro-ya was as it had been, he said, except the toilets, some of which he had changed to the modern style to accommodate visitors from places like Tokyo, Osaka, and Nagoya. In the rooms, there were no televisions, no telephones, or anything electronic except for the lights, which had been installed, reluctantly, by his grandfather.

That night I was called down to dinner in a small room, my only companion a newspaper writer from Tokyo. Amid servings of river fish, mountain vegetables, grilled mushrooms, rice, and beer, we talked over our surroundings and made plans to walk over the pass to the post town of Magome the next morning. He would write a story about Tsumago and this short section of the Kiso Road upon his return.

The following morning, my new friend and I ate an early breakfast of fish, miso soup, vegetables, and rice, and then headed out for our hike. The innkeeper had kindly supplied us with the small bells travelers wear to scare off the black bears that inhabit the mountains; the weather was cool and the sky perfectly clear, and we chatted all along the path—again, the old Kiso Road—up over the low but steep mountains, ringing our little bells in full faith and stopping to rest every thirty minutes or so. Much of the old road wound through dark cedar forests, the road itself often made of the original large, rough stones called *ishitatami* laid down in the early 1600s, and marked here and there with ancient stone statues of guardian gods.

Finally we breached the top of the pass and walked down into the village of Magome, another hamlet that had been preserved, then burned down, then rebuilt mostly as it had been for over a hundred years. Here my writer friend took a bus to start his way back to Tokyo, and I took another minibus back to Tsumago. That night, after a lengthy bath in a traditional wooden tub overflowing with near-boiling water, and then dinner, I took a short walk through the village to see overhead more stars than I could remember had ever existed. With no street lamps and only a few lights shining from the occasional inn, the darkness—and quiet—were nearly complete. Back tucked in under my futon, I thought for a little while about the many different travelers who had rested here in this room since the inn was established so long ago—pilgrims, samurai accompanying their lords , traveling priests, poets and townspeople just out for a lark. With such company in mind, I fell into a deep and undisturbed sleep.

THE FOLLOWING PAGES are an account of a hike I took along the Kiso Road during the autumn months of 2013. The Kiso Road—*kisoji* 木曽路 in Japanese[1]—runs about sixty miles through central Nagano Prefecture and mostly follows first the Narai and then the Kiso River (traveling from north to south) through the granite forest-covered mountains of that same name.[2] It is the heart of the longer 340-mile road, the Nakasendo (also called the Kisokaido), which stretches from Tokyo to Kyoto. It is called a "road,"[3] and it often runs parallel to or on Highway 19 but just as often wanders into the mountains as a smaller paved road or just a narrow path of dirt or ancient paving stones. The Kisoji has been in use for perhaps over two thousand years, although it was most popular as a thoroughfare during the sixteenth through nineteenth centuries when travelers walked, rode on horseback, or were carried in palanquins through the mountains, along scary suspension bridges built on cliffs overlooking the swift river and over the steep passes.

It is not too easy to get lost on this road, although it can be done, as I have sometimes proved; markers are posted along the way in Japanese, English, Korean, and Chinese because the authorities do not want to go looking for you. There are also eleven villages, established in 1601 as post towns, about six to seven miles apart, where the modern hiker can stop for the night in traditional inns, just as his counterparts did far back into the past. And, although there are sometimes quick gains and drops in elevation as the road meanders through the mountains, even people in moderate shape can walk the entire sixty miles in less than a week. My preference, however, is to take it at a much more moderate pace. The beauty of the mountains and rivers, and the experience of the traditional baths, cuisine, and bedding in the inns are not to be rushed through. For this particular hike—I've walked the road a number of times over the past decade and a half—I took three weeks. Had time permitted, I would have taken more.

This account is also somewhat of a story map, much as is described in the opening quote. Over the years that I've traveled the Kisoji, I've been lucky enough to meet with a number of people—innkeepers, coffee shop owners, farmers, Buddhist priests, and hikers like myself—who have generously shared their knowledge of the rich history, traditions, and folklore of the area. Because of the antiquity of the road—it is first mentioned in a Japanese chronicle dated 701—there are also a number of books that describe not only the geography and topography of the road, but also local spots inhabited by ghosts and animals like foxes and badgers that bewitch the unwary traveler, or places famous for some romantic or tragic event. These guidebooks, many of which were written in the early 1800s when the Kiso Road was at its greatest popularity, were intended for the inquisitive traveler of those times and are still wonderfully informative. Poets and journalists, such as Basho and Shiki, also loved traveling the Kiso Road, and, along with excerpts from the early guidebooks, I have included a number of their poetic impressions—many by Santoka, the shabby Zen priest/haiku poet/sake drinker, whose presence I felt constantly.

In this way, the territory covered here is not just geographical, the time line not limited to late October/early November of 2013, and the hike not mine alone.

I HAVE ALSO been fortunate to have many times walked the Kiso Road with friends—artists and writers for the most part—whose energies and perceptions have greatly added to my understanding and enjoyment of this, my favorite place on earth. Thus, I owe an extreme debt of gratitude to Emily and Henry Wilson, Gary Haskins, Robertson Adams, Kate Barnes, Shinji Kobayashi, Mayumi Tison, Chris and Kathy Knight, Daniel Medvedov, and Ginny and Tadashi Takemori. There are also those whom I met along the way whose extraordinary knowledge, generosity, and kindness made my travels all the more interesting, comfortable, and informed. Their name is legion, but a few of them are Hida Isao, Ando Mineko and Ryuji of Nakatsugawa, Ted Taylor, Fujiwara Yohei, Shirota Hirosuke, Mr. and Mrs. Tsuchikawa of Narai, Hotta Fumiko, Dr. Okuhara Tasuku, Jinmura Haruo, Imai Yasuko, Murakami Atsushi and his gracious wife, Imai Akinori, Ichikawa Yutaka and Mihoko of the Yakiyama no Yu, Matsuse Yasuko, Uegaki Ryoko, the *o-kami-san* of the Isami Ryokan in Yabuhara, and Fujiwara Yoshinori.

There are no words that could ever express my gratitude to my friend and mentor, Ichikawa Takashi, whose erudition in Japanese literature and culture, expertise in mountaineering, and companionship have nearly defined my experiences in Japan over the last forty-five years. His generosity beggars the word itself. I would like to note that I still have the superb climbing boots he had made for me in 1968, although, to my chagrin, I did not take them along on this trip.

I would also like to thank the fine people at Shambhala Publications—especially Beth Frankl, John Golebiewski, and Jonathan Green—for suggesting this project and supporting me throughout. Their patience seems to be without limits.

Finally are my deep bows of thanks to my professors of Japanese language and literature, the late Dr. Richard McKinnon and Prof. Hiraga Noburu, both of whom have traveled roads far deeper into the world described in these pages than I will ever go.

Walking the Kiso Road

Introduction

魚相造乎水、人相造乎道。
相造乎水者、穿池而養給。
相造乎道者、無事而生定。
故曰、魚相忘乎江、人相忘乎道術

[Confucius said,] "Fish are made for water; men are made
for the Road.[1] Those who are made for the water immerse
themselves totally in ponds and are nourished by them.
Those who are made for the Road live carefree and tranquil.
Thus it is said, 'Fish do not think about the water,
and men do not worry about the Road or how to walk it.'"

—*Analects,* Chapter 6

A HIKE ON THE KISO ROAD will take the traveler much farther
back than the seventeenth and eighteenth centuries, when a number of the still-extant inns along the way were established. The
road was first mentioned in an early historical chronical, the *Zoku*
nihongi, in an entry for December in the year 702, which states,
"For the first time, the Kiso Mountains in the province of Mino
have been opened." A following entry in the same chronical for
the year 713 implies both that the road had been completed and
the reasons why it should be traveled: "The paths in the Kiso area
of the provinces of Mino and Shinano [later called Nagano] are
steep, and the round trip is difficult. Therefore, one takes the Kiso
Road."

The road, however, is much older still. Traveled extensively and
settled here and there by the hunting and fishing Jomon people

1

who inhabited Japan from about 11,000 B.C.E., it was before that, no doubt, a trail for the bear, deer, wild pigs, and other animals that still inhabit the region today. The population of the area decreased during the ensuing agricultural Yayoi period (200 B.C.E.–250 C.E.) and the following court-centered periods, but by the tenth and eleventh centuries, villages and hamlets had grown up along the river bank, and certain areas had come under control of a samurai gentry living in mansions that supported Buddhist temples and some commerce in lumber. Eventually, daimyo and local warlords staked their claims as hereditary owners of the lands, barriers were put up along the road to control mercantile activities, robbers, and, to some extent, military incursions, and traffic increased. Finally, the eleven towns along the Kiso—from north to south: Niekawa, Narai, Yabuhara, Miya no koshi, Kiso Fukushima, Agematsu, Suhara, Nojiri, Midono, Tsumago, and Magome—were firmly established by the middle of the 1500s, adding a certain amount of security to the traveler who chose to take the route along the deep valleys and dark forests through which this road winds.

IN OCTOBER OF THE YEAR 1600, the Eastern forces under the command of Tokugawa Ieyasu defeated the Western forces loyal to the Toyotomi clan in one of the most important battles in the history of Japan. The result of this victory—mostly won on the misty, rainy plain of Sekigahara—was the pacification of the country after nearly two hundred years of a steadily declining Ashikaga shogunate and debilitating civil wars. Ieyasu would soon be named shogun, and Japan, more or less, would be under his control, more or less, because the provinces and fiefs of the country were still ruled by the daimyo, or hereditary warlords, whose loyalty could never be taken for granted.

The movement of troops being thus a major concern, Ieyasu soon developed an infrastructure of five major roads, the *gokaido*

五街道, which monitored and controlled military and official communications between the capital of Edo (now Tokyo) and Kyoto, and also the outlying provinces. These roads were to be maintained by the local daimyo whose fiefs they passed through, but provincial barriers were banned and replaced here and there by those designated by shogunal decree. Post stations were designated—248 for the entire gokaido system—every five or six miles, depending on the topography and conditions of the road.

In 1635, Ieyasu's grandson, the shogun Iemitsu, instituted the *sankin kotai* system to further tighten the central government's control over the provincial daimyo. This system required all the daimyo of Japan to reside in Edo every other year for a year to several months and, further, required their wives and families to live permanently in the capital as virtual hostages.

This, along with the great improvements in the economy, had a profound influence on the gokaido in general, and on the Tokaido and Nakasendo—the two most used of the five roads—in particular. The samurai making up the daimyo's retinue often numbered in the thousands, and inns, shops, teahouses, and other accommodations in the post towns increased accordingly. Concomitantly, with the increased safety and improvements in the conditions of the roads, the newly more affluent common people could travel confidently as well.

In the end, by the eighteenth and nineteenth centuries, what had been intended as a system of tighter control ended in an unprecedented freedom of movement for a great portion of the population. A road culture had been created that would influence literature, the visual arts, cuisine, and the cross-fertilization of ideas—many of which we think of as classically Japanese even today.

THE TOKAIDO AND THE NAKASENDO—BOTH running between Kyoto and Edo—were the most popularly traveled of the gokaido.

The Tokaido—flat, mostly level, and by far sustaining the most traffic—paralleled the eastern seaboard and involved the crossing of twelve rivers and a few larger bodies of water, such as Ise Bay and Lake Hamanako, as well. Regardless of the necessity of ferry crossings, which sometimes involved rough waves and long waits, the weather was relatively warm and pleasant, and thus the Tokaido was a preferred route.

On the other hand, the Nakasendo, and especially the Kiso Road section, ran through deep mountain valleys and along treacherous cliffs and was often cold even during the early and late summers. Nonetheless, it was the favored route of the imperial family, the nobility and their princesses, and the family of the shogun. The most famous journey along the Nakasendo is, perhaps, that of the princess Kazunomiya, who traveled to Edo in 1862 to marry the fourteenth Tokugawa shogun, Iemochi. Her retinue consisted of some twenty-five thousand men, which backed up some of the more difficult passes for weeks. The mountains and rivers, the forests and mists the young princess would have seen as she peeked from behind the blinds of her palanquin comprised much of the same scenery we see today. But being the daughter of an emperor, and surrounded by thousands of noblemen, noblewomen, and samurai, she would have missed most of what the common folk took interest in and what we encounter as we walk along with our tiny bear bells and walking sticks.

THE ROAD

Although the gokaido were controlled by the Tokugawa shogunate and its representatives, maintenance was delegated to the local daimyo. Thus the condition of the provincial segments reflected upon the prestige of those daimyo and was duly noted by dignitaries both foreign and domestic. In this way, the roads tended to be kept neat and passable, whether consisting of dirt, gravel, or stone pavement. The shogunate also ordered that a line of trees—pines and cypresses—be planted along the highways, ostensibly to protect travelers from the sun during the summer and the cold winds in the winter. This may have had a military objective as well, however, as the trees would have been cut down across the roads to impede invading armies on their way to Edo. Again, local maintenance was required.

To mark progress along the roads, *ichirizuka,* or one-*ri* (about two and a half miles) markers, were placed in clear locations, often next to a pine, cherry, or zelkova tree. The Nakasendo had about 130 of these markers between Edo and Kyoto, and a number of these can still be seen on the Kiso Road section today.

Although the road now ascends and descends in elevation, there are many level stretches that make for comparatively easy walking. The *toge,* or "passes," however, while not particularly high in elevation, are steep and often narrow, and would cause backups in progress for days or even weeks as some retinues were composed of hundreds or thousands of samurai, pack horses, and carriers. Thus, there were often specified resting places, relay stations and teahouses along the way where travelers could stop to catch their breath but could not stay overnight.

Bridges were built only with permission from the shogunate government. They sometimes spanned a river but more often were the frightening *kakehashi,* or suspension bridges made of wooden planks held together with thick vines that followed a cliff overhanging the rushing current beneath. Bridges were sometimes washed away by floods, and both revenue and building materials were difficult to come by. Today, with the advent of the national highways and the new "car culture," the original bridges are all but gone. The site of one of the most famous, however, the kakehashi near the northern entrance of the post town of Agematsu, is clearly marked, and the traveler can imagine the trepidation with which these bridges were approached.

PEOPLE ON THE ROAD

Everyone, it seems, was on the gokaido during the Edo period (1600–1868). As official roads, of course, first in priority were the daimyo, who either rode on horseback or were carried in palanquins, and their innumerable attendants (on foot except for the higher-ranked samurai) on their way between their home provinces and the capital. Spearmen bearing blades covered with fur took the lead of these retinues, which included cooks and even wooden tubs for the daimyo's baths. As noted, there were also members of the imperial court traveling as emissaries of the emperor or accompanying a princess betrothed to a shogun. There were the further dignitaries of the Korean ambassadors and the representatives of the Dutch settlement in Kyushu.

Then there were the common people: merchants of every stripe, from representatives of the large commercial houses (their merchandise went mostly by sea) to traveling peddlers carrying their goods on poles over their shoulders; pilgrims on their way to Ise Shrine, the Thirty-Three Temples on the island of Shikoku, or the Zenkoji, a famous Buddhist temple in the city of Nagano; blind masseurs, or *zattou,* who specialized in massage, moxa, and acupuncture; *goze,* the blind female street singers who, traveling in groups of two or three, played the samisen and sang songs from classical tales, like the *Heike monogatari;* and country doctors, or *inaka isha,* who identified themselves by pulling their hair back into ponytails, wore black jackets, carried sun umbrellas, and hoisted their doctor's bag wrapped in large cloth kerchiefs on their backs. There were also subscription monks soliciting contributions for their construction or repair of temples, and *komusou,* monks who wore large straw hats that covered most of their faces and begged for alms while playing a bamboo flute. These latter monks were supposedly members of the Fuke sect of Buddhism but were suspected to be spies for the government and were often given wide berth. The fact that they carried short swords was not lost on either locals or other travelers.

Other than the huge daimyo retinues, however, the most numerous travelers on the gokaido—and particularly on the Nakasendo and the Tokaido—were the *yuusan ryokyaku,* people traveling for pleasure. These people could be townsmen, farmers, groups of women who had left home for a while with or without the permission of their families, shop boys who simply decided to take a break from work, and even children who begged for alms along the way. Most of these claimed they were on pilgrimages, and many were, but the fact was that "pilgrimages" had become a sort of recreation—an excuse to get out of humdrum daily life and to see places other than home. Not much was required in equipment, after all: a good pair of straw sandals, a paper umbrella or an oiled paper coat against the rain, and perhaps a straw mat to lie on in an emergency. These and almost everything else could be supplied in the numerous shops and teahouses along the way—and still can be.

POST TOWNS

The road within the post towns was fixed at a width of fifteen to thirty feet, while the length of the post towns ranged from a little over four hundred feet to nearly eight thousand feet. When Kaibara Ekiken passed through the Kiso Road in the early seventeenth century, he reported that the size of the towns varied from 28 households in tiny Magome to 130 in Kiso Fukushima. Throughout the following two centuries, the towns would prosper or decline depending on economic, political, or environmental factors.

Despite the differences in size, however, the structure of the towns was basically the same. The Nakasendo/Kiso Road was the main or only street in town and was usually lined on both sides by shops, inns, and food stalls. The road itself, however, often meandered this way and that in what was called a *dako* 蛇行, or "snake crawl," sometimes taking sharp L-shaped turns. This pattern—along with the square-shaped *masugata,* gates often constructed with stone walls at the entrances and exits of the towns—was designed to confuse and slow down an invading army or a hostile force passing through on its way to Edo.

As the post towns were originally designated as way stations for daimyo on their way to and from Edo and to facilitate shogunate and merchant communication, each one provided a *honjin,* an officially appointed inn for dignitaries, and a forwarding agent to take care of supplies, called a *toiya.* The honjin, some of which survive today, was accoutered with gates, ceremonial entrances, and the very best of rooms where the most exalted personages could either rest or stay overnight. Often, a shrine or Buddhist temple was situated at the rear of a honjin in case a quick evacuation was necessary in times of war. A *waki-honjin,* or lateral honjin, was nearby in the case of an overflow of dignitaries. Naturally, the honjin was reserved for those of the highest status.

The common people also needed places to stay, and as travel became more and more popular during the Edo period, inns—called *hatagoya*—sprang up in increasing numbers. Such inns were basically divided into two categories. The *meshimori hatago* provided, along with lodging, prostitutes under the guise of serving girls. Inns were initially limited to two such "waitresses," but this number was found to be difficult to enforce. Hatagoya that did not provide these services were called *hirahatago* and catered more to women travelers, married men, and samurai who, no doubt, were under the watchful eyes of their daimyo. Many inns employed *tome onna,* women who coaxed, and sometimes forcefully pulled, travelers into their establishments.

On the Kiso Road, some of the inns established during these times are still extant and in business. Today, the inns are divided into two types: the *ryokan,* usually more expensive and where meals are often served in private rooms, and the *minshuku,* less formal and where the guests dine in a common room.

The *toiya,* often the busiest place in the post town, was a relay station, providing horses for daimyo, their samurai, and the nobility. It also functioned to make arrangements for sending baggage on to the next station, and its services were also available to merchants and travelers who could afford horses and palanquins. The men who managed the toiya wore a three-quarter-length jacket and a sort of suit pants, and had the special right of carrying a sword. It was their responsibility to make sure there was always a sufficient number of horses and men to transport the myriad travel equipment deemed essential by the daimyo, a job that sometimes necessitated bringing in corvée laborers from nearby farming communities.

Buddhist temples and Shinto shrines, some of them much larger than one might expect for the relatively small populations, provided (and still provide) for the religious needs of the townspeople. The Zen sect dominates most of the temples in the Kiso, and, while we associate Zen with religious austerities and long periods of meditation, the priests' main functions were to carry out funeral ceremonies for the deceased, take care of the mortuary tablets of the ancestors, deliver Buddhist and Confucian homilies to locals, and keep an eye out for their general welfare. The central government approved of and helped to support these temples and expected the priests to stay in line with its policies, especially those of acquiescence to the Tokugawa shogunate.

The post towns offered the authorities an institution, if not to regulate, at least to oversee the high volume of traffic on the road. Passing by these towns was strictly prohibited, and those travelers on horseback or riding palanquins were required to hire new transportation at each location. In this way, each town was guaranteed a certain amount of business regardless of its size or population, and every traveler was at least assured of a look at another aspect of the road.

A WORD SHOULD BE SAID about modern coffee houses in Japan, and especially on the old Kiso Road. The first coffee house opened in Japan was in Tokyo, in 1888. This venue, the Kahiichakan, apparently included such amenities as baths, billiard tables, and writing desks, but—perhaps due to mismanagement—eventually went out of business. Coffee, however, was in Japan to stay, and the coffee house soon replaced the old teahouse as a place to either meet friends or just decompress alone. Japanese coffee, regardless of its origin (Jamaica or Kenya, for example), is usually rich and tasty, and great care is taken in its brewing. For the modern customer who arrives before ten o'clock in the morning, a "morning set"—a hard-boiled egg, a thick-cut piece of toasted white bread with butter and jam, and perhaps a dollop of fresh potato salad or coleslaw—is usually available. The shops are generally comfortable and friendly, and the customer is never encouraged to move on in any way. They are designed for your pleasure, sometimes specializing in classical music, sometimes in jazz, and so forth. There is almost always something to read nearby, be it a newspaper or magazine, and there are coffee shops that specialize in manga, where these graphic novels literally line the walls.

Coffee shops are an institution in Japan, to be found in the smallest towns and villages, and in this way it is perhaps not surprising that they now appear in even the most traditional post towns on the Kiso Road. As with other preserved buildings that make up the towns, the coffee shops are often located in a former Edo- or early-Meiji-period shop of some sort and retain all the traditional atmosphere of the earlier business. The proprietors of these shops are always friendly and helpful, and, in some cases, their families may have lived in the village, and even in the location of the shop, for hundreds of years. Thus, they are always good sources of information or just congenial talk and not to be thought of as interlopers.

BARRIERS

From the twelfth century and perhaps earlier, local and provincial lords established *bansho*—barriers, or checkpoints—at various places along the roads to control troop movements, regulate commerce (especially the illegal export of lumber), discourage brigandage, and generally to keep an eye on the movements of the provincial population. With the establishment of Tokugawa hegemony in 1600, these *bansho* were ordered to be removed along the gokaido and were replaced here and there by *sekisho*—larger barriers and checkpoints controlled by the Tokugawa and operated by their hereditary representatives. Some of these sekisho were indeed imposing edifices. Built in deep valleys or where cliffs ran parallel to a rushing river, they included stout wooden gates at the entrance and exits manned by armed soldiers. Weapons stocked in the sekisho included firearms, bows and arrows, heavy wooden staves, and barbed spears to catch those unfortunates who tried to push their way through. Miscreants, the insane, and criminals were shackled or tied up, their fates to be decided later by the magistrate.

The main purpose of the sekisho, however, was to ensure the security of the Tokugawa government in Edo. Thus, its most important functions were to stop any movement of firearms into the capital and to watch for the passage of women—the daimyo's wives and daughters—on their way back to the provinces. Any attempt to remove these women from Edo, where they were more or less hostages, could be seen as a warning sign of a rebellion by their husbands or fathers. For this reason, the passage of women through the sekisho was discouraged in general, and even young effeminate-looking boys were physically checked—often at very close range—though they be accompanied by farmers or merchants.

To pass through the sekisho, permits or passports (*tegata*) were required, which, for the common people, were issued at any number of places, from clergy at temples and shrines, post station officials, or, in some cases, innkeepers. As the number of travelers increased during the middle and late Edo period, *tegata* were more and more easily acquired, and the sekisho guards would sometimes allow passage through the gates even without one. This was especially true when large groups of people arrived, supposedly on a "pilgrimage," and the checking of every document would impede more important work.

This leniency is illustrated in the case of the Edo-period haiku poet Koshigaya Gozan, who was stopped at a barrier while traveling the Kiso Road.

> At the outset, I was on foot and was about to pass through the barrier at Fukushima in the province of Mino. The guard asked what my profession was, and I responded that I was a teacher of haiku. "If that's the case," he said, "prove it with a verse and I'll let you through." Just then, a cuckoo cried [and I recited],

> At the barrier, in no way
> would they let me through;
> [then,] a cuckoo!

Easing travel even further were the byroads that skirted some of the sekisho, which could be located by asking the locals or sometimes consulting a guidebook. In some cases there were holes in the sekisho walls that a person or even a group of people might squeeze through at night—the gates were open from six in the morning to six at night—and so go on their way.

All in all, the fifty-three barriers along the gokaido were established to provide some stability to the country—first, political, then commercial and social. Although travel by the common people was not encouraged by either the central or local governments, the general leniency shown to them at the sekisho did nothing to stem the tide. Finally, with the Meiji Restoration in 1868 and the eventual dissolution of the domainal clans, many of the barriers were torn down as remnants of an older age, while those that remained standing or were rebuilt as historically important became wonders for an ever-increasing number of travelers.

YESTERDAY AND TODAY

Travelers have journeyed along the Kiso Road for nearly a thousand years—for inspiration, aesthetic pleasure, or the sheer joy of walking through mountains and rivers of outstanding beauty. In the twelfth century, the poet-priest Saigyo walked through on his way to the then capital of Kamakura, writing classical poetry and performing religious austerities. In the seventeenth century, the Buddhist priest Takuan and the haiku poet Basho traveled into the Kiso, taking notes and composing verse after verse. Later there were the poets Buson, Yayoi Yuya, Shiki, and Santoka, Kaibara Ekiken (the physician, philosopher, and writer), and the famous wood-block print artists Hiroshige and Eisen. The writer Ikku Jippensha had his comic characters Kita and Yaji go down the road in his *Zoku hizakurige,* and Yoshikawa Eiji famously depicted the swordsman Miyamoto Musashi not only walking the Kiso Road, but meditating under a waterfall that modern hikers still delight in visiting today. These are only a few of the well-known travelers who have passed through wide-eyed at the scenery, sat down and counted their blisters, visited the famous Zen temples, drank cool water from the mountain streams, and spent happy nights at the local inns. Japanese hikers and tourists walk the same road today: some just to get out of their urban areas and appreciate the deep mountains, the autumn foliage, and cherry blossoms in the spring; others to experience the living traditional Japan that was the daily fare of their not-so-distant ancestors.

To say "the same road," however, is not quite accurate. Over the millennia, the path has been covered or swept away by earthquakes, typhoons, flooding rivers, or the works of man. Even as recently as a few years ago, a short length of the road was covered by a landslide, and hikers have had to take a detour. On some maps, sections of the road will be designated as "the old Kiso Road," but, when considered in terms of centuries, one may well ask, "Old compared to what?" The traveler will find that the scenery has not much changed, however: the mists still hang in the folds of the mountains, the clear water of the Kiso River still rushes over monstrous boulders, the passes are no easier to climb than they were for the samurai accompanying their mounted lords, the old pick-me-up *gohei*—grilled mochi covered with sweet miso sauce—can still be found in local food stalls, and travelers can still bed down in an inn that may have been established shortly after Columbus discovered America. This is the Japan that many tourists hope to see when they deboard their international flights just outside of Tokyo or Osaka but never leave the enticing, interesting but distractingly modern urban areas. What Walter Weston, the British missionary turned mountain climber, wrote in 1917, remains true today.

> There is a popular impression, widely prevalent to-day, that a traveler bound for Japan in search of the primitive and the picturesque, which are there to be found combined to a degree unknown in any other country so easy of access, unless he hurries quickly hither, is likely to find his opportunities vanished and his quest proved a fool's errand. And yet, happily, there are still to be found, by those who know where to seek them, not forty-eight hours distant from the very heart of the empire itself, remote and lonely valleys whose old-world ways, quaint superstitions, and primitive institutions almost compel the belief that one has, in less than two days' journey from Tokyo, executed, as it were, a leap backward from the twentieth century to the tenth.
>
> —*The Playground of the Far East*

IT SHOULD BE ADDED that most of the post towns described in this book can be reached by the local Chuo-sen railroad line, taken either from Tokyo or Nagoya. For those towns that the railroad has not reached, minibuses and taxis are available. I would agree with Thoreau, however, that he travels best who goes afoot. Blisters and rain-soaked boots aside.

The Upper Kiso

1 Edo (Tokyo)

道中は	Do not think
自由をせんと	"I'll go as I please!"
思ふまし	when taking a journey.
ふ自由せんとすれば	Rather, think, "I may have some problems,"
自由ふぞ	and you'll be free as a bird.

—Yasumi Roan

TRAVEL TIME between Miami, Florida, and Tokyo, Japan, is about seventeen and a half hours—plenty of time to contemplate what I was getting myself into. My plan was to walk solo the sixty miles through the Kiso Mountains, stopping over each night at one of the traditional inns along the way—a hike I had done a number of times before and always loved. Trapped now on the plane, however, with its cramped seats, food of questionable origin, stale movies, and a one-and-a-half-seat-sized passenger on my left gave me ample time to question the wisdom of this trip. My neighbor was asleep, slumped onto my shoulder because the man next to him was even bigger and not inclined to share his armrest. I was thankful at least to have an aisle seat.

At one point, my bunkmate woke up and informed me that he was in the military and on his way to the Philippines. When I asked him where he was last stationed, he said Uzbekistan, which, he noted, must be somewhere in Europe because everyone there seemed to speak German. I mulled over this interesting piece of travel information and decided not to disturb him with any more small talk. He had a long way to go to Manila, which is, perhaps, somewhere in South America.

FINALLY OUR PLANE made a smooth landing into Narita airport. I zipped through customs—nobody really wanted to look through my well-used backpack—and purchased my ticket for the express train into Tokyo. During the one-and-a-half-hour ride, I fell asleep a number of times, only to wake up with a jolt. Familiar sights emerged through the dark of the window—red paper lanterns in front of *izakaya,* neon signs in Chinese characters, and from time to time a *konbini* (convenience store), such as Lawson or Circle K. Eventually we pulled into Shinjuku Station. I navigated my way through a labyrinth of corridors and caught a cab to Kagurazaka.

Kagurazaka is an old hilltop geisha district now filled with traditional bars and restaurants that cater to those who are affluent or have generous expense accounts. My cabbie stopped at the red-orange and white Buddhist temple at the top of the hill, and after paying the fare to the amiable driver, I slipped into the narrow alleyway across the street and followed the uneven cobblestones to the Wakana Ryokan. There is a little garden just inside the gate, and just past the threshold of the sliding front door, a cat sat motionless on a low wooden table. A tiny terrier, yapping bravely, came out to greet me, followed by the proprietress of the inn.

The Wakana, a small traditional inn, is well-known as a *honkaki ryokan,* or writer's inn. It was founded in 1954 by a then-famous and very beautiful actress and is now run by her younger sister. This year marked its sixtieth in operation, and the proprietress (or *o-kami-san*) had been thinking of closing it down. There was a hue and cry from former patrons, however, who include novelists, playwrights, movie directors, television writers, and others, many of whom spent untold hours here through the years, drinking up sake and ambiance in equal parts as they wrote their masterpieces. Years ago, I was doing some writing myself here one night, half listening to the muted happy laughter coming from the nearby drinking establishments, when there was a sudden short tremor. The laughing stopped immediately, but for less than a minute, and then resumed. People come to this long-established neighborhood to enjoy the company of their friends and a few cups of sake. Something as common as an earthquake was not going to ruin anyone's good time.

It was still early evening, so I left my backpack in my room (actually two rooms: one of six tatami and one of four-and-a-half) and headed back up the alleyway in search of a place to eat. Nearby I found a cheap udon restaurant, where I ordered a bowl of the thick noodles and a small bottle of draft beer. I hadn't noticed him when I sat down, but next to me was another foreigner, a cheerful young Brit who had saved his money working in the publishing business and was taking a six-day holiday, his first visit to Japan. He was staying in a hostel and after three days in Tokyo would take a night bus to Kyoto. Finishing our meal, we walked out onto the bustling street, where we bid each other farewell.

A night bus to anywhere is for the young, I said to myself, and hurried back to the quiet comfort of the Wakana. There, I changed into my *yukata* and headed for the *o-furo*, the traditional Japanese bath. This one has a floor and steps of river stone, and one wall mounted with sheets of volcanic rock. In this sort of lodging, the necessities are provided for the bather—shampoo, conditioner, body wash, tiny thin towels, toothbrushes, and tiny tubes of toothpaste. I sat on a wooden stool, scrubbed down, and rinsed by repeatedly filling a wooden bucket with hot water and dumping it over myself. My ablutions complete, I sank slowly into the smallish marble tub.

ひとりの湯 が こぼれる
A bath
for one,
overflowing
—Santoka

The water in the traditional Japanese bath is generally quite hot—one toe in at a time. The bather comes out the color of a lobster, and bed is about the only option. Fortunately the ryokan staff had spread out my futon for me while I was soaking. I crawled under the covers by 10:30 P.M. and was sound asleep by 10:31.

JET LAG WAS DOING ITS WORK every hour on the hour, but I persisted and so slept on again and off again, with worries about the walk, my own competence, and fitness. In the bath earlier, I had had a good look at my pitifully skinny legs and wondered how they were going to carry me over the passes and on the longer stints of the road. But too late now—they would have to do.

By half past six, it was useless to try for any more sleep, so I got up and dressed, slipped out of the inn, and strolled the wet streets toward the Café Volace, across from the Buddhist temple. People were already off to work, and a woman was busily setting up to sell flowers on the sidewalk. It was a quiet crowd at the Café Volace: well-dressed office workers and salarymen were reading their newspapers or looking at iPads and iPhones to the sounds of Pachelbel's Canon in D. This is the Japan of the present day, the Japan I would not see again for three weeks.

By the time I finished my café au lait, it was raining, so I bought a cheap umbrella before crossing the street to the temple and making a one-hundred-yen offering and a prayer for my safe return. I also bought a small tiger *o-mamori,* a protective charm, just as insurance. The lady taking my money from behind the window informed me that this temple had been founded in 1595 by the soon-to-be shogun, Tokugawa Ieyasu (on whom James Clavell based the character Toranaga in *Shogun*). This temple belongs to the Nichiren Buddhist sect but is dedicated to Bishamonten, the most powerful of the Buddhist "Guardians of the Four Directions" and one of the "Seven Happy Gods" (*shichi fukujin*). Clad in armor and holding a spear, he wards off hostility to Buddhism and protects the Dharma (and, I hoped, lone walkers on ancient roads).

As the lady and I talked, others—young and old, well dressed and those in very plain clothes—walked up the steps in the light rain, bowed and prayed, and reverently tossed a few coins into the offertory. Bishamon would be busy that day.

On the way back to the Wakana, I bought some flowers from the lady on the sidewalk for the o-kami-san. The little dog announced my return to the inn and accompanied me back to my room, where breakfast awaited: grilled salmon, eggplant, spinach, lightly fried tofu, rice, herbs boiled in a light soy sauce, miso soup, and green tea, all enticingly arranged on a red lacquerware tray.

After a quick cold-water shave, I fussed with my backpack, settled up, said good-bye to the o-kami-san, and headed up the hill for a parting cup of Japanese joe at my favorite coffee shop in Tokyo, The Bronx. The owner, goateed and clearly a survivor of the hippie days in Japan, remembered me from my last visit years ago and, in the course of our conversation, warned me that not one, but two typhoons were moving from the southwest toward the Kiso area and would probably hit the following day. This was not encouraging news, but I thanked my host, took my leave, caught a cab back to Shinjuku Station, and boarded a train to Shiojiri, whence I would set forth, whatever the weather, onto the Kiso Road.

But first the long ride out of Tokyo: once a small fishing village, now one of the largest cities in the world. Tokyo is largely a maze of cement and steel—huge buildings crowded together, heavy traffic, the streets always filled with people. From the train window, however, I could see small forests or wooded areas here and there, surrounding local shrines or temples—green spaces for the gods and buddhas, as if to evoke their primeval origins. These are reminders that Tokyo was a castle town that grew to envelop the surrounding villages, some of which still retain their old local dialects from long ago. Here and there were persimmon trees full of orange-colored fruit, even in Tokyo.

Then, rather abruptly, we were passing through mist-filled mountains, covered with trees, bright with changing leaves and the beginnings of autumn. Then we continued through Kofu, located in a sort of topographical basin famous for grapes and other fruits and for having been the home base of Takeda Shingen, a great general during the Warring States period (*sengoku jidai*). Shingen was on his way to unifying Japan when was he was felled by either a bullet or a sudden illness—accounts vary. His clan was then all but annihilated under the incompetent leadership of his son. Had Shingen lived to realize his ambition, Kofu would likely be the capital of Japan today, and Tokyo (or Edo, as it was called then) just another remnant of a feudal-period castle town.

At last, our train pulled into Shiojiri, home to seventy thousand or so souls. Shiojiri was also a busy post town on the old Nakasendo, but there is still an air of the truly ancient to the place, which has been inhabited since the Jomon period (11,000 B.C.E.–200 C.E.). My inn here—just a short walk from the station—would be the Asahi Ryokan, established over one hundred years ago and a popular stop for travelers on the old post road. To keep up with the times, the old building—a three-story wood and clay structure—was demolished some years ago and rebuilt as a modern inn with both Japanese- and Western-style rooms and accommodations.

Too late to make a reservation for dinner, I walked through drizzling rain under the half-light of street lamps until finding the brand new Appleland department store. Incongruously, Halloween decorations and pumpkins were everywhere, and signs posted on the huge glass windows wished me a "Happy Hallow-een!" Halloween is enthusiastically celebrated in parts of Japan; children and adults wear costumes and have parties, affording the adults yet another occasion on which to drink. Trick or treat? The Japanese do love festivals, which now include Christmas and St. Valentine's Day, but most are held during the summer months, so a new late-fall *matsuri* must be a welcome addition to the calendar.

After a dinner of Neapolitan pizza, the Appleland café specialty, I walked up the stairs to their bookstore, where I found and pur-chased a children's book of the Confucian *Analects,* beautifully illustrated in pastels by local artists. It would add to the weight of my pack but was too lovely to resist, and I wanted something to read; I could always pass it on to someone I met on the way.

Back in my room at the ryokan, I pushed aside the ubiquitous flyers advertising pay-per-view girlie programs, sat down at the desk, and flipped open my new book.

> Nothing is more apparent than that which is hidden;
> Nothing is more manifest than that which is indistinct.
> Therefore the Gentleman restrains himself when alone.
> —*Doctrine of the Mean*

With this Confucian bit of advice lingering in half thoughts, I climbed into my comfortable bed—the last Western bed I would sleep in for a while. Tomorrow my trip would begin in earnest, and I would need all the rest I could get.

2 On the Road

*On the first day of a journey, step out firmly but calmly, making
sure that your footwear has adapted itself to your feet. For two
or three days after starting out, rest from time to time, so that
your feet won't hurt. At first, anyone will be impatient and walk
along restlessly without a thought of taking a break. But if your
feet start to hurt, you will suffer a good bit during your trip. At
any rate, it is essential that you are attentive to your feet at the
very beginning.*

*The things that you carry along on a journey should be very
few, no more than what you can put into a small pack. You may
think that you need to bring a lot of things, but in fact, they will
only become troublesome.*

—Ryoko yojinshu (1810),
A Collection of Essential Travel Tips

JET LAG AND SLEEPLESSNESS plagued me again, so I gave up
at around four thirty and checked the weather report on the television. A sober-looking young reporter soon informed his early-
morning viewers that typhoons number 27 and 28 would probably "sandwich" Nagano Prefecture (and so the Kiso Road) within
a few hours, bringing plenty of rain. Also, there had been another
earthquake off Fukushima, with a magnitude of 7 (something),
and tsunami warnings had been posted along the northeastern
coast.

So maybe "plenty of rain" was the least of my worries.

27

Shutting off the broadcast, I turned back to Confucius and found this entry:

知者楽水 The wise man takes pleasure in water.
仁者楽山 The man of humanity takes pleasure in mountains.
知者動　 The wise man moves.
仁者静　 The man of humanity is at rest.
知者楽　 The wise man enjoys.
仁者壽　 The man of humanity has long life.

There would be plenty of both water (synonymous with "river" in classical Chinese) and mountains in the Kiso, so the wise man and the man of humanity should both be in their elements.

Breakfast was served in the dining room, as Asahi Ryokan is technically a *minshuku* rather than a ryokan. Four other early risers were having their meal at another table, but they were busily reading newspapers as they ate, and I did not bother them with conversation. Breakfast included a nice piece of grilled salmon, very lightly poached eggs, a dish of *chikuwa* (a kind of tube-shaped fish paste with the firmness of a pancake—really, quite tasty), mushrooms and tofu, a dish of chopped lettuce with one *umeboshi* (a bright red, sour pickled plum), rice with seaweed strips, green tea, and then coffee. With that, I was ready for the road.

Back up in my room, I repacked my backpack. Though in theory I espouse Stevenson's "travel light" dictum, my pared-down packing list contained a shaving kit; a small sewing kit; a travel alarm clock; aspirin, Advil, and vitamins; a compact first-aid kit with Band-Aids and Neosporin; toothbrush and toothpaste; tiny grooming scissors; a miniature flashlight; a hand mirror; five long-sleeved undershirts; six pairs of underpants; one second shirt and an extra pair of Levis; a sweater; three pairs of wool socks; one pair of silk socks to wear as liners under wool socks; one catalog-fresh poncho; writing materials; one Japanese-English dictionary, one English-Japanese dictionary, and one Kanji-Japanese dictionary. Ah, yes, and my new book of Confucius.

Having lingered too long over that last cup of coffee at breakfast, I found at the station that I had just missed the local train to Hideshio, the true starting point for hiking the Kiso, and that the next one would not be along for another two hours. Since the cab fare to the Hideshio station was not too much, I decided not to wait. My cab driver had been brought up in the area and knew it well. He seemed pleased that I was doing this walk and offered me a good hiker's map, the same one that was already in my coat pocket. We wound over small roads through the rainy hills and talked a little about the history and the sheer beauty of the Kiso Road, which he had walked a number of times. I told him that this would be my fourth time to do this hike, and he nodded and smiled approvingly. "Arukiakiru koto wo shiranai, ne." You never get tired of walking it, do you?

After twenty minutes or so, my new friend turned into a narrow lane—the old Nakasendo—and dropped me off at the path leading up to the tiny Hideshio railway station, which is actually nothing more than a bench under a three-sided, roofed shelter. He was concerned about the rain, but I assured him that I was well prepared, and after he drove hesitantly away, I spent the next twenty minutes trying to figure out how my new poncho unfolded and fitted over me and my pack.

Hideshio is a small town, a village really, only a few minutes' walk from the old post town of Motoyama, dotted with a few private residences and a large gas station on the other side of the main road. I was on a smaller road, the old Kisoji, the heart of the Nakasendo. By the side of the road down the way from the little train station, there is still an old one-ri stone marker about two and a half feet tall, marking that the traveler is sixty-one ri to Edo (modern-day Tokyo) and yet seventy-one ri to Kyoto.

According to the 1805 edition of the *Kisoji meisho zue,* "Along the Kiso Road, there are many shops that sell various animal skins. These are especially numerous between Niekawa and Motoyama [i.e., Hideshio]. There are a great number of people who try to sell bear livers to passing travelers, so you must be wary." And, in Ota Nanpo's *Jinjutsu kiko* 壬戌紀行 of 1802, we find, "There is a stopping place called Hideshio where they sell bear hides; but there is nothing [like this?] east of here."

Since ancient times in both China and Japan, bear gall has been thought to cure various ailments, no doubt because of the bear's strength and life force and the view that the liver is the general of all the organs of the body, controlling the nervous system and perception. Small black bears still abound in this area, and I have encountered them twice between Hideshio and Niekawa; but both times, they took one look at me and ran down into the ravine. Bears have poor eyesight, and I wonder now if, seeing the blurred bulk of me and my backpack, they mistook me for a large alpha bear. The bear researcher Douglas Peacock wrote about encountering grizzlies several times in Yellowstone National Park and raising his arms a foot or so above his hips to convince them that he was bigger than he really was. It worked for him, and perhaps my pack worked for me, but this trick is not fail-safe, and I wouldn't advise relying on it.

This time there were no bears, but the rain and wind were working in tandem to soak every part of me that wasn't covered by the poncho. In less than an hour, I reached the stone monument that marks the true beginning of the Kiso Road, engraved with これよ り南木曽路—"From here south, the Kiso Road." It is here that the mountains begin to close in on either side, the valley deepens, and the traveler is struck by the atmosphere of the place that will be present every step of the journey. In his novel *Yoakemae* (*Before the Dawn*), Shimazaki Toson wrote the lines known to everyone who lives or travels the Kiso:

The Kiso Road runs entirely through the mountains. In some places, the road goes along rocky cliffs; in others it follows the banks of the deep Kiso River for some distance; in still others, it winds around the foothills of the mountains and enters the valley. This single line of a road penetrates an area of deep forests.

Though it was late in October, the autumn leaves had just begun to turn at the edge of the mountains, suggesting the astonishing array of colors that would soon be everywhere: the red, purple, yellow, and brown of the maples and other deciduous trees, punctuated by the green of the cypress, pines, and cryptomeria. Here and there, persimmon trees were conspicuously full of their orange fruit, hanging from already leafless trees, and the Narai River now appeared, now disappeared down in the ravine to my right. What is here little more than a large rushing stream flows out of the Kisokomagatake Mountains and becomes Japan's longest river. Eventually merging with three other rivers, it becomes the Shinano River at the border of Echigo and flows into the Sea of Japan. At this northern end of the Kiso, however, the Narai River is narrow enough to hide beneath the autumn leaves; only its gurgling, chuckling sounds remind the traveler that this is just the beginning. The river and the traveler still have a long way to go.

From Hideshio, the Kiso Road runs along National Highway 19, as it does in stretches all the way to Midono, the ninth post town. The Kiso Valley was a convenient place to run the highway—and the Chuo-sen railway line—when transportation was being developed from the late 1800s through the mid-1900s, and little consideration was given to the historic and scenic value of the area. I was thinking of just this as trucks zoomed by, bringing gusts that ripped my hat from my head. Off I ran back after it, my poncho flapping in the wind and rain.

After a short while but a steady incline, the Kiso Road veers off onto a narrow side road and into the hamlet of Katahira. There was a Zen Buddhist temple here, established in 1575, with the rather romantic name of Ochakuji 鴬着寺, or "the temple where the nightingale arrives." Wandering around, I could find nothing that looked remotely similar to a traditional Buddhist temple, however, and I finally rang the doorbell at one of the few houses here to ask for directions. A smiling gray-haired man opened the sliding door and, in response to my query, took an umbrella and walked out with me through the now-light rain. On a small rise just a few steps away sat a residential-looking building with only a wooden placard over the door and a few small stone monuments next to the entrance to give any hint of its purpose. The priest only drove out here once a month or so, my guide explained, adding that the name of the temple, Ochakuji, has to do with the small mountain behind the temple, Umeyama (Plum Mountain). Plums and nightingales are poetically connected in Japan, and the saying "uguisu no ume mitsuketa yo"—"like a nightingale that has discovered a plum"—means something that is extremely convenient and as desired.

A wooden image of Jizo—the patron bodhisattva of children, small animals, and travelers—is enshrined inside the temple. Jizo is also known as the bodhisattva who goes through the six ways (or realms)—those of hell beings, hungry ghosts, animals, human beings, angry gods, and heavenly gods—guiding their inhabitants away from their distractions and back to the Dharma. He is often depicted carrying a staff topped with six iron rings, with which he breaks down the gates of hell. The rings also jingle as he walks, warning small animals of his approach so that they can get out from underfoot. Unfortunately the entrance to the temple was locked, so the Jizo here would remain a mystery.

Taking my leave with a deep bow, which my guide returned despite the umbrella, I carried on, and at the edge of the hamlet passed an old stone statue of the Horse-Headed Kannon—a deity who protects animals (especially horses and cattle). Kannon is the Buddhist bodhisattva of compassion, and statues of the

Horse-Headed Kannon are found all over the Kiso Valley, a region famous since ancient times for its excellent horses.

Lichen-covered statues of *dosojin*, deities in the forms of an old man and woman, also appear at the roadside to protect travelers, as do statues of Jizo. Frequent encounters with these ancient spirits cheer and uplift, and provide a form of company to the solitary walker.

Finally the road took a turn down to the national highway, and the mountains, which up to this point had been gradually closing in on both sides, seemed suddenly to snap shut. In just a few minutes, I crossed the thoroughfare and walked into the post town of Niekawa.

COURSE TIME

Hideshio to Niekawa-shuku: 8 kilometers (4.8 miles). 2 hours, 30 minutes.

3 Niekawa

旅人と	*"A traveler"*
我名よばれん	*let me be called;*
初あしぐれ	*the first autumn rain.*

—Basho

W‍HEN the samurai physician and philosopher Kaibara Eki-ken passed through Niekawa in 1685, he only noted, "It is a rather confined, squeezed-together village of some sixty to seventy houses and a barrier station. From here, the road goes uphill." The author of the *Kiso meisho zue*, 120 years later, informed his readers that

> a long time ago, there was a hot spring here, and for this reason it was called Niekawa, or Boiling River. [The kanji 贄 (*nie*) actually means "gift" or "offering," but is homophonous with the verb "to boil or cook.] . . . It is a town of quite some wealth, with people's homes scattered here and there.

In 1839, Okada Zenkuro, a samurai serving the Owari branch of the Tokugawa at their Edo mansion, was sent on a secret mission to investigate conditions in the Kiso Valley in order to revise rice allotments. In his report, the *Kisojun koki*, we can see that the population had grown—no doubt due to the heavy traffic on the Nakasendo—and he wrote the following:

> There are some 227 houses here concerned either with commerce or agriculture, and the population stands at 1,016 people.

There are in this post town some fifty-nine people who work both agriculture and commerce, and are thus involved in trade. For this reason, in years of bad harvest, with some prudence, there are not as many people starving to death or leaving the area as there are in Narai or Yabuhara. In the traffic of officials and horses, the post town officials are excellent, scrupulous men, and there are no hindrances in going forward.

Nowadays, Niekawa is a small town of a few shops and private homes. Once a thriving post town, it partially burned down in 1782 and then suffered a number of other fire disasters, which eventually dried up the small streams of water for common use that went through the town. Niekawa was entirely destroyed by fire in 1930 and then rebuilt to appear mostly as it does today, the important waki-honjin being replaced by a sake shop. The inns that once attracted weary travelers are gone altogether.

The main point of interest in Niekawa is its small barrier, or *bansho*. Built on an elevated place only a few paces down a slight incline from the post town, it was originally established by the Kiso clan in 1335 to control all movement through the Kiso Valley. By the mid-1600s, however, it was being operated by vassals of the Yamamura magistrates of Kiso Fukushima to monitor the passage of women, firearms, and Japanese cypress. The bansho is positioned such that it would be difficult to pass unnoticed by officials stationed there, but the building itself is small—really only three rooms and a tiny office. Large rocks secure its shingled roof against the winds that come through the valley. An array of weapons is displayed on the walls, and when walking through the close quarters, one understands that the inspection was a deadly serious business.

By the time I arrived at the barrier, I was soaked from hat to boot and stopped to rest on the raised wooden veranda once trod by the magistrates' watchmen. Here, I transgressed one of the cardinal rules of the *Ryoko yojinshu*: "When resting at a tea house, do not sit down dangling your feet with your footwear on. Even if it is just for a short time, take off your footwear, sit on the bench or porch, and rest with proper posture. Strangely enough, this will lessen your fatigue." To my good fortune, the lady taking admission fees noticed me sitting there and came out to talk; she then kindly made me a cup of hot coffee. As I warmed myself with the coffee, she offered me some ginger-coated black-sugar candies, most of which I put in my coat pocket for later. As we sat and chatted, my benefactor revealed that she was a local and spent some time teaching elementary school but loved the mostly quiet job of tending the barrier. Tourists came on the weekends, especially in autumn, but otherwise she was often alone, reading contentedly and looking out to the north—from which direction I had just come—with its beautiful view of the valley.

We talked for a while about the area—she was especially interested in the Neolithic Jomon people who lived here once—and she invited me to look through the small museum of Jomon and other historical artifacts of the area. By this time, however, the warming effect of the coffee had worn off, and I was feeling a slight chill, so we bowed our good-byes. Many times in the days that followed, dipping into my pocket for a refreshing taste of sugared ginger, I wondered at the Japanese people's great gift of kindness to strangers.

It was a short walk through the town, and after about two hundred yards the Kisoji winds around to the right and passes what was once a bubbling spring that was the community's source of water. Today it is just a large cistern with a zinc roof, but still all-important for the life of this isolated village. Along the way, I looked for the Shingon Buddhist temple that, according to the *Kiso meisho zue*, was established here in 806. Eventually abandoned and allowed to become dilapidated but rebuilt in 1616, either nothing remains of the temple or I completely missed it in the rain. Sadly, the hot spring of long ago is also gone.

After a winding walk through an area dense with Japanese cypress, juniper, and cryptomeria, the road once again joins the national highway and then splits away from it, joining it again at the hamlet of Nagase. In 1755, the author of the *Kisoji junranki* stated only, "Nagase—one house. The owner is a doctor who possesses various specific remedies, one of which is a wonderful medicine for lumbago."

Today Nagase boasts at least a few more homes, a convenience store, and a souvenir shop selling items of lacquerware and wood. Its biggest draw for me, however, was the Nagase noodle shop, a restaurant outfitted with solid cypress slab tables, smoke-darkened rafters, and a huge heater with a pipe chimney in the center of the room. Just outside and visible through the windows is a tiny stone garden punctuated with small trees and a pond filled with koi (carp). I had last eaten here with my friends Gary Haskins and Robertson Adams when we walked the Kiso Road as a sort of moving bachelor's party a few weeks before my wedding. Gary, a life-long friend, is a potter and artist, and we were constantly losing sight of him along the trail as he stood enraptured among the huge trees that grace the Kiso Valley. Robbie, a graphic designer, had lived in Tokyo years before, and he also loved this view of Japan that his previous experience had not afforded him.

After a very satisfying meal of thick udon noodles and tempura shrimp, I walked out to find that there was still a light rain. Donning backpack and struggling with the poncho, I was off once again down the national highway. Shortly, the Kisoji turns off to the right, and after a time, there is a sign informing the traveler that he or she is approaching the Hirazawa Lacquerware Hall, a museum displaying the methods and tools of lacquerware production, goods made here over the years. Gary, Robbie, and I spent a good bit of time here on our walk, looking at the various items on display and sampling the chestnut coffee they make here, but today, I carried on.

The village of Hirazawa, a few minutes' walk from the museum and with a main street lined with shops, has been a center of lacquerware production since the Edo period. With its cold temperature and deep valleys, it is not suited for agriculture, but it is surrounded by an abundance of lumber. Everything from expensive heirloom-quality items with gold and silver inlay to folk ware bowls and trays for everyday use are available here, but unfortunately, most are too large to cram into a full backpack. However, it is worth a visit to the museum and/or a walk through the town just to appreciate the simplicity and elegance of these beautiful and quintessentially Japanese wares.

Near the museum entrance, there is a large stone monument engraved with a verse by the famous haiku poet Basho:

送られつ
送りつ果ては
木曽の秋

Being sent off,
in the end, sending them off:
autumn in the Kiso.

Basho wrote this verse when he passed through the Kiso in 1688, and the magistrate of Kiso Fukushima had the monument erected. A copy of the monument also stands at Shinchaya, the southern entrance to the Kiso Road.

Turning to the right, I found myself on narrower and narrower roads and eventually came out onto a willow-lined path along the Narai River. Passing the miniscule U-Life Coffee Shop, loud and lively even at a distance, and crossing the bridge over the river and then the Chuo-sen railroad tracks, I passed the railroad station and walked into the post town of Narai.

COURSE TIME

Niekawa-shuku to Narai-shuku: 7 kilometers (4.2 miles). 3 hours.

4 Narai

ただ一人	*Totally alone*
北斎の絵の	*I walk right through*
中を行く	*Hokusai's print.*
木曽の山路の	*Summer at dusk*
夏の夕ぐれ	*on the Kiso Road.*

—Yoshii Isamu

THE FAMOUS JAPANESE WOODBLOCK artists of the nineteenth century—Hokusai, Eisen, and Hiroshige—had already discovered the Kiso Road to be redolent of the past, and walking into the post town of Narai, the twenty-first-century traveler is struck with a similar sense of stepping backward in time rather than forward. Old wooden buildings with latticed doors, narrow overhanging balconies and eaves, and large wicket bumpers line both sides of the one narrow main street. The names of the ryokans and minshukus are engraved on ancient wooden placards above the entranceways, and small eating establishments, many of which have been beckoning pilgrims and other travelers for over a hundred years, are interspersed with shops selling lacquerware and other traditional items, perfect souvenirs for those waiting at home. Above one shop entrance is the traditional large ball made of cedar leaves and twigs, advertising it to be a place where the local sake, *Sugi no mori* ("Cedar Forest"), is brewed. Farther down the street, pure, fresh water gushes from two bamboo pipes into a public cistern with long-handled bamboo cups for drinking.

Large, potted white and yellow chrysanthemums are set at almost every door. Narai was established, at least officially, around the year 1500, and during the Edo period was known as "Narai of a thousand lodgings," perhaps an exaggeration—Kaibara Ekiken found only a hundred houses when he walked through—but the place still has the air of a thriving and hospitable nineteenth-century town. Ota Nanpo passed through Narai in the spring of 1803, and noted,

> When you look over the station of Narai, there are plum trees, cherry blossoms, early-flowering cherry trees, and apricot trees with their branches mixed together, giving you the impression of the true heart of spring. In the inns there are many useful articles for sale: bowls, lunch boxes, sake cups, round clip boxes, etc.—all of them the workmanship of this area. . . . The post town is quite prosperous.

This was not always the case, however; when Okada Zenkuro visited the town less than forty years later, he left this account:

> This post town, like Yabuhara, is at a high altitude, so there are few rice fields or vegetable gardens. Moreover, the climate is quite cold, so harvests are meager. Because there is little in the way of agriculture, the inhabitants of both the post town and nearby Hirazawa have made a living by becoming craftsmen in works of Japanese cypress and lacquerware. In years past, such profits have been made from these goods that the population increased, and a good business was made from these crafts. Nevertheless, just recently, such goods have not been in favor in either Edo or Osaka, and business was poor; thus, in the famine of 1837, many people either died or left the area, making the official business of the post town difficult to carry out. Gradually, there was a loss of both population and houses despite official aid, and disastrous fires have occurred as well. Five temples have been lost in these fires, and with the great destitution, the rebuilding of main temples remains in doubt.

Wet, tired, and hungry, I stepped into Hokusai's print of Narai and headed straight for the Matsuya Sabo, a tidy coffee shop housed in a building that has been there since the last fire 180 years ago. There I was greeted by the proprietor, Mr. Imai Akinori, and his two toy poodles, Piano and Chopin. Imai-san is the ninth generation of a family that has lived at this location for over 300 years. His outgoing and friendly personality, full shock of white hair, and neatly trimmed goatee and beard all conspire to give the impression of a larger man than he actually is.

As he prepared my coffee and one of his wife's apple tarts, he told me that in earlier years, the family business had been making accessory combs—not the utilitarian cedar combs so popular today, but the decorative lacquerware combs for women's hair, bought as souvenirs for lovers and wives. An engraved wooden sign carved four generations ago stands just inside the entrance to the shop. Imai-san explained that around the early 1930s the old hairstyles went out of fashion, and no one seemed interested in the combs anymore. In addition, the Chuo-sen railway line was built, and although there is a local station here, fewer people stopped in Narai, making it a lonely place until the 1970s. It was a only a few decades ago that he decided to open a coffee shop here, re-creating in it the atmosphere of an old Kiso teahouse where travelers could stop to rest and regain their spirits.

Imai-san is a great talker and quite knowledgeable about the history of Narai. He was quick to show me some of his historical artifacts: his favorite (and mine) being an old Edo-period Chinese-Japanese dictionary, a real treasure, and he kept an anxious eye on it as I thumbed through the pages.

After an hour and one more excellent cup of coffee, I had revived sufficiently to head out from the Matsuya Sabo and look for the inn where I would spend the night.

Following Imai-san's directions, I retraced my steps and soon found the sign for the Tsuchikawa-ya, a relatively new inn opened only fifty years ago. No one answered my knock at the entrance, so I opened the sliding door and found a long narrow corridor leading to another building—the inn itself—behind the first. Stepping inside, I called out a hesitant, "Gomen kudasai" (something like "Excuse me, I'm here"), and was greeted by a smiling Mrs. Tsuchikawa, who, after introductions and pleasantries, showed me to my accommodations on the third floor. The two tatami rooms were neat and clean, and the sliding glass balcony doors opened to a beautiful view of fall colors and mists moving through the folds of the mountains. The bath and toilet were on the second floor.

> 宿にとりて一に方角ニ雪隠三に戸じまり四には火のもと
> When taking an inn
> at first get your bearings,
> then find the toilet,
> how to secure your doors,
> and finally, the source of fires.
> —*Ryoko yojinshu*

Japanese tea and rice cakes were soon brought in on a lacquerware tray and placed on the low table in the center of the room. I had carried my soaked boots in with me and now placed them in front of the gas heater atop some old newspapers provided by my hostess. Pulling a small pillow filled with buckwheat hulls from the closet, I lay down to rest.

Sometime later, Mr. Tsuchikawa came up to introduce himself. Imai-san, a good friend of his, had called to tell him of my journey and of my love for the Kiso Road. It turned out that Tsuchikawa-san, a shy but loquacious man, is a scholar of the road and has a library full of books concerning its history and geography. He generously offered to lend me any of them while I stayed at the inn, and I picked out two from the crowded bookshelves: a copy of *Konjaku nakasendo hitori annai* (A Guide to Traveling Alone on the Nakasendo) by Imai Kingo and *Shinanoji no haijintachi* (Haiku Poets on the Shinano Road), a book on the haiku poets who had traveled through the area. The first included a guide of the Kiso Road, with ancient and modern maps and quotes from journals and travel guides from the Edo period; the other devoted an entire chapter to Santoka, the ultimate walker and my favorite Japanese poet of all. I opened the books and, entranced, barely noticed as Tsuchikawa-san slipped out of my room and downstairs to start preparing for the evening meal.

Before I knew it, it was time for dinner. This took place in a small dining room on the first floor, the only other guests that night being a young couple from Tokyo. The three of us ate quietly, watching the television news of typhoons 27 and 28 and the earthquake. The typhoons had caused considerable damage, including landslides and the destruction of homes on the outer eastern islands, but the earthquake's effects had been minimal. Everyone was concerned, however, not least because it took place off the coast of Fukushima, not too far from the newlyweds' home in Tokyo.

Dinner was grilled *iwana* (a river fish, *Salvelinus pluvius*), three different dishes of vegetables and mushrooms, rice, soba (buckwheat noodles), miso soup, thin slices of beef served *shabu shabu* style (dipped briefly into boiling broth and then a sauce at the table), and Japanese tea. It was delicious, but as often in Japanese inns, the quantity was more than I could handle. After eating more than I thought possible, I excused myself and wished everyone a good night.

After another hour or so with Tsuchikawa-san's books, I headed down to the second floor for a deeply relaxing Japanese bath in a rectangular cedar tub. This is a treat that few Japanese were able to afford in the past. Of the five types of trees for which the Kiso is famed, four are of the cedar and cypress families. Exportation of these trees had been strictly limited during the Edo period and slightly before, when Hideyoshi, the most powerful man in the country, wanted to ensure that no castles would be built larger than his own in Osaka. Even the locals were forbidden to use much lumber, and illegal removal and use of it sometimes resulted in the loss of a hand or execution. The general policy was "one branch, one head."

After a long soak, I returned to my room, read a little more Confucius, and found one of my favorite lines:

朽木不可雕也。糞土之牆、不可杇也
You cannot carve a rotten piece of wood;
You cannot plaster a wall made of dung.

Yes, I should study those books a little more, I thought, and drifted off to sleep.

———

烏が鳴くと天気が変わる
When crows caw, the weather will change.
—Old Japanese saying

CLEAR SKIES! At six thirty, I opened my sliding glass doors to see the mountain right in front of me, full of red, orange, gold, purple, and green in the early-morning light. Large Japanese crows (*karasu*) were cawing somewhere in the distance. There was some soreness in my calves as I stood out on the balcony; one of Mr. Tsuchikawa's books showed that yesterday's steady climb to Narai, elevation 3,104 feet, had amounted to some 500 feet. Somehow I had passed the first day in moderately good shape.

But now I limped down to the first floor for a breakfast of three tiny fish, eggplant with miso sauce, various vegetables, scrambled eggs, mashed potatoes, tomatoes, miso soup, rice with seaweed, Japanese pear slices, apple juice, and Japanese tea. Each portion was presented on its own small dish, as such meals always are. The conversation turned to Santoka, and Mr. Tsuchikawa recited several of the poet's haiku, including one reportedly written in Narai.

水はおのづから
里へわたしも
若葉ふみわけて

The river goes on by itself;
I, too, on my way to the village
walking through the young leaves.

After just barely finishing my ample breakfast, I climbed back up the stairs to read a little more from the book of haiku poets on the Nakasendo. Santoka loved the Kiso and, in all of his peregrinations around Japan, found time to walk it three times—the last time in 1939 at the age of fifty-eight, a year before his death.

And so I was off to the Matsuya Soba for coffee, an essential to start the day. It was early, but Imai-san was already making coffee and bantering with some elderly women tourists who had also come in for their own jolt of java. There was no sign of Chopin or Piano, but the shop was filling up and getting lively.

Narai is mostly a line of shops, inns, and minshukus, with dark wooden latticework on almost every building, narrow balconies, and roofs overhanging sliding doors, and it has the feeling of a very old town. It is really just a single street, with its five large Buddhist temples—which were rebuilt and have prospered, despite Okada Zenkuro's pessimistic report—behind the shops on the western side of town. Slightly farther to the west behind one of these temples is the Taihoji, an elevated hill where remain the earth configurations of a castle and a moat. This is the site of Narai Castle, governed by Narai Yoshitaka during the mid-1500s. The exact date of the castle's construction is not known, but archeological remains indicate a fortress that measured about two hundred feet east and west, and over three hundred feet north and south. Some stones and a dry moat are all that remain.

The blue-green Narai River, studded with rocks and boulders of every size, runs along the east side of the town. It is spanned by an old-style single-arched bridge, about one hundred feet long and eighteen feet wide. Although it was constructed with three-hundred-year-old cedar beams and supports, it was actually built in 1991, with grant money from the national government for the renewal of cities, towns, and villages. There was once another bridge here, noted as the "Great Bridge of Narai" in the *Kisoji jun-ranki* of 1755, but which no doubt washed away in one of the many floods that have occurred here. This morning, as I passed the bridge on my way to the Taihoji, the sun shone brightly against the cedar planking, a few pedestrians were doing their best not to slip on the lingering morning dew, and dragonflies still filled the air.

I entered the grounds of the Taihoji, a Zen Buddhist temple, the main hall of which dates from 1658, though the temple itself is said to be much older. It is a large, low structure of whitewashed clay and dark wood trim, and as you enter the grounds, you are greeted by a stone statue of the bodhisattva Jizo, holding a small child in his left hand and a staff in his right. Two bigger children cling to his robes, and he stands on a lotus petal. Jizo (Ksitigarbha in Sanskrit) is a sort of patron saint of children who have died young and babies who have died in the womb. Tradition has it that such children must gain merit for themselves and their parents by building votive markers with small stones. This they do on a sandy riverbank called the *sai no kawara,* but every night an evil old demon, the *sozu no kawara no uba,* comes and knocks the markers down. Eventually, Jizo comes to console the children, saving them from further torment and leading them to salvation. Although Jizo does not fit neatly into the Zen concept of emptiness, his statues are found at many Zen temples throughout Japan, including those on the Kiso Road.

At the edge of the mountain directly behind the main hall is a garden, created in 1725, consisting of an arrangement of stones interspersed with trees. In the lower part of the garden is a pond with an island in the middle. The design is said to be based on an early Japanese gardening book, the *Sakuteiki.* As prescribed in this text, there are guardian rocks on the far side of the pond, before which is placed a large, slender triangular stone, to evoke the lines of a statue of Kannon, the bodhisattva of compassion. The island in the center of the pond is a collection of large stones arranged in the shape of a turtle with head, feet, and tail, at the same time suggesting the Chinese ideograph for "heart/mind."

At the time of this visit, the once-famous garden was a mess. As I stood on the temple veranda trying to envision its former beauty, I fell into a conversation with a couple, the Tanakas, who were apparently trying to do the same thing. Eventually, the head priest's wife joined us and explained that the last workmen hired to "trim" the garden had been amateurs and pretty much butchered what was considered a local treasure. It would take years to reconstruct it, she said sadly, and would cost more than the temple could afford, but they had started to work on it bit by bit.

The priest's wife was looking glum with this account, and the Tanakas and I were at a loss for words. We all moved into the temple's main hall, where we were shown a large wooden placard engraved with calligraphy by the famous swordsman/statesman/artist Yamaoka Tesshu, who visited the temple in 1889. A big man, well over six feet tall, Tesshu was a Zen adept, an extraordinarily talented swordsman, a womanizer (whose wife finally put a stop to his wandering ways by threatening him with a butcher knife), and a friend, advisor, and drinking partner to the emperor Meiji. All of this dynamism and life force seemed to be reflected in his calligraphic work now hanging near the dais of the main object of worship, a statue of the Buddha Shakyamuni.

Presently, the Tanakas and I took leave of our hostess and walked around to the side of the temple where there is a three-foot headless stone statue of Maria Jizo, discovered buried in a thicket in 1932. There are Maria Jizos and Maria Kannons throughout Japan, and several in the Kiso Valley. Looking like Buddhist bodhisattvas but meant as devotional representations of Jesus's mother, Mary, they were worshipped by "hidden Christians" after Christianity was forbidden by the central government in the late 1500s. The statue at Taihoji depicts a woman holding a child, who is grasping a lotus flower, a Buddhist symbol. Inside the flower, however, is a small cross, indicating the true intention of the sculptor. That the statue's head is missing may reflect the anti-Christian sentiments held by the people who threw the statue into the weeds long ago, or it may actually have been mistaken for a Buddhist object of worship. Many Buddhist statues also suffered this vandalism during the Meiji period, when State Shinto was advocated and Buddhism was officially condemned. Headless or not, it is a remarkable sculpture and, by the number of coins placed in the offertory, appeared to be revered by Christians and Buddhists alike.

After chatting a while longer, I bid good-bye to the Tanakas and walked back up to the Senninji, a temple on the northern edge of town. The cedar and cypress woods are thicker and darker in this area, an ancient section of the Kisoji that runs through the forest, and in a tiny glen, there is an arrangement of the "Two Hundred Jizos," small, worn, lichen-covered stone statues of Jizo, Kannon, and other deities. The Senninji itself belongs to the Shinshu Buddhist sect and is famous for its *unari ishi,* or "moaning stone," a four-foot-tall stone on the road just at the entrance to the temple grounds. Tradition has it that, many years ago, this stone would start moaning as soon as night fell. This was disconcerting to the people who lived near the temple, so someone drove a nail into the stone, but this had no effect. As a last resort, sake was poured liberally over the stone, and all the moaning ceased.

As I scrutinized the rock, looking for the nail—it's supposed to be there still—a cheerful old gentleman in a black mourning coat and a bowler derby approached me and offered other theories as to why the rock cried.

1. It was going to be moved to another location and didn't want to go.
2. A priest kicked it and hurt its feelings.
3. It wasn't the rock that was crying, but a tanuki—the trickster, shape-shifting raccoon-dog of Japanese folklore—that was hiding behind the rock, waiting for someone to come up with the idea of sake.

The gentleman was then joined by three or four friends and their wives—all of them on a temple visit, I supposed—and I noticed that one of the men, bearded and smiling, was holding a large, boxed bottle of sake. He looked at the rock, looked at me, broke into an even broader smile, and seemed to hold his bottle of sake with a slightly tighter grip. Then, unaccountably, everyone was smiling.

> When strange things happen like suddenly being lost on the road, or it's suddenly getting dark, or a river appearing where there wasn't one before, or a closed gate blocking the way where there was no gate previously, calm yourself down and be aware that this is the handiwork of foxes and tanuki. Smoke a little tobacco and rest . . . Thus the deception of the fox or tanuki will be undone.
> —*Ryoko yojinshu*

On the way back to my ryokan, I noticed a signboard by the side of the road I had missed before, with a message written in chalk in both Japanese and English.

道はその日その日の生活の中にある
The Way is nowhere else but in our daily lives.

ACCORDING TO THE very first article in the *Angya jo,* or Basho's *Rules on Pilgrimages,*

> You should not sleep twice in the same inn. Your thoughts should be on a mat that has not yet been warmed.

I was not particularly anxious to leave the warm, friendly, even collegial atmosphere of the Tsuchikawa-ya; but in deference to the wisdom of the great poet and traveler Basho, I set out for my new lodging at the Ise-ya, just a short walk away in the middle of Narai.

The Ise-ya was established in 1818 and once housed the commission agency for the waki-honjin. The old section of the building is of traditional architecture, with high ceilings and smoke-darkened rafters, and the old sign advertising it as a place of rest—御休泊—still hangs above the entranceway. The new section of the inn, where I was to stay, is modern but retains traditional elements of tatami, futon, and opaque sliding windows. In the center of my room, the customary low table was already set with tea and rice cakes, and within moments I settled in. Common bathrooms, both modern and traditional, are down the hall.

At about four thirty, I was advised by the proprietor to go ahead and bathe, as there were a number of guests and time would be limited later on. The tub itself turned out to be an old wooden one, with hot water gushing continually from a large faucet. Having washed and rinsed myself well, I slid into the tub and allowed myself to sit and soak only as long as I thought I could without inconveniencing other guests. I remembered Yasumi Roan's advice:

> If you go to take a bath in an inn where there are other guests, be sure to follow the instructions of the innkeeper. In a busy inn it is possible to mix up the proper order in using the bath, and that can easily cause an argument. At such a time, look carefully at the other guests; if someone appears to be of high status, let him take his bath before you. At any rate, being mistaken about the order of using the bath can result in fights. In all cases, if you will be reserved in all matters when on a journey, you will often be better off.
>
> —*Ryoko yojinshu*

Dinner was announced a few hours later, and all the guests went down to the large dining hall on the first floor. The room reflected the age of the place with sliding paper doors, carved wooden designs (*ranma*) over the doors, latticed walls, and wooden beams. Several long low tables were lined with thin cushions for sitting, and we were each brought large lacquerware trays filled with small dishes of the local cuisine. I requested a small portion of sake, which was presented in an elegant unglazed earthenware sake bottle and cup. There were about fifteen of us, and I sat at the end of the table with two Japanese-Brazilian ladies, one of whom spoke Japanese, on vacation from São Paulo. They had come all this way, they said, to find something of their roots and had found what they were looking for in Narai, and particularly at the Ise-ya. The woman who spoke Japanese was at a loss to express just exactly what that was, but I imagined I could understand her feelings quite well. The atmosphere of the Japanese inn seems to encompass that of the country as a whole; and if someone were able to spend only a single night in Japan, my recommendation would be to stay in the most traditional ryokan available—regardless of the price.

By this time, I was feeling the effects of the hot bath, huge meal, and the sake, and so finished off the last drops in my *guinomi*, excused myself, and headed to my room and the futon. The next day was going to include a tough hike, and I wanted to be ready for it. My last thoughts wandered back to the Senninji, the dark woods beyond it filled with smiling tanuki in bowler hats, and I was happy when sleep finally came.

5 The Torii Pass ELEVATION 3,600 FEET

When people are passing along roads deep in the mountains and through the fields, and are accompanied by fellow travelers, bears and wolves will hide when they hear human voices. . . . A single traveler will not be talking, however, so wild beasts sleeping by the side of the road will be alarmed by unexpectedly encountering a human being, and will bite him. Such events will not occur in broad daylight, but will happen on a night road. Thus, when walking deep in the mountains or through the fields far from human habitation, you should step along making a sound by striking the road in front of you with a prepared bamboo staff. You can also smear cow manure on the bottoms of your footwear as you walk a mountain road, and wild beasts, snakes, mamushi *[a kind of very poisonous snake: Agkistrodon blomhoffi] and poisonous insects will be afraid to approach you.*

—*Ryoko yojinshu*

B REAKFAST at the Ise-ya was surprisingly simple, compared with the evening's feast: dishes of pickled white radish, miso soup, the usual variety of mountain vegetables, and an unending supply of coffee. The meal was served in a smaller room in the old building near the entrance, and the guests sat at unvarnished wooden benches and tables. I sat across from an elderly couple, Mr. and Mrs. Katayama, who turned out to be from Tokoname, a city famous for its burnished reddish-orange pottery, and the

55

hometown of my *shakuhachi* teacher decades ago, Hirano Yoshi-kazu. The Hirano family was quite well-known in traditional Japanese music circles, as not only Hirano-san but also his wife and mother were masters of the thirteen-string koto. The Kataya-mas had been friends of the Hiranos and knew them quite well. They reported that, sadly, my teacher had passed away just a few years ago at a relatively young age. We talked on for a while about the Hirano family and Tokoname pottery, had our photos taken together, and departed with silent bows.

Studying the koto and shakuhachi with the Hirano family had been my introduction to the musical traditions of Japan. Their patience with a foreigner struggling to master even the basics of these two remarkable instruments was impressive, and they always corrected me with an inclusive and good-natured laugh. My teacher's passing was sad news, but just the mention of his name brought back memories of times spent in their welcoming house cluttered with musical instruments, the Japanese tanger-ines that were always there for refreshment, and cup after cup of green tea.

Thanking the inn's proprietor, I shouldered my backpack and walked south through Narai, passing the Upper Ton'ya Museum, which displays various historical documents and artifacts of daily life during the post-town period. Constructed in 1840, the museum is rich with the atmosphere of long ago. Farther along is the Chozenji, a large Zen Buddhist temple constructed some-time between 1362 and 1368, and rebuilt in 1592. This temple also houses a minshuku for travelers who don't mind fewer comforts and a quieter, more ascetic ambiance. At the path to the temple, a lady bent almost double with age but shouldering her own back-pack greeted me with a "Gambatte, ne! Gaijin-san!" ("Carry on, hey! Mr. Foreigner!")

At the very edge of town is a large Shinto shrine, the Shizume Jinja, surrounded by a woods of large, dark cedar trees. Com-pared to Zen temples, which often are well-manicured and open to the light, Shinto shrines are set deep in the shade of trees and huge rocks, exuding a feeling of mystery and the unknown, and informing you that you are entering into the world of the *kami,* or gods. The story behind this particular shrine is as follows:

> About nine hundred years ago, around the time of the emperor Konoe (1141–55), there lived an extremely virtuous man, Naka-hara Kaneuji, whom the village people revered. When Kaneuji passed away, the people cherished the memory of the man's virtue, built a shrine commemorating him at the top of the Torii Pass, and for nearly 420 years celebrated him as the shrine's deity. In the second month of 1583, however, the armies of the Kiso clan and the Takeda clan clashed at the Torii Pass, and the shrine burned to the ground. Soon thereafter, Narai Yoshitaka enshrined Kaneuji at the foot of the pass, and this was the establishment of the Shizume Shrine.

There is, however, another tradition. The *Kisoji meisho zue* states that "an epidemic spread throughout Narai between 1615 and 1624, and the construction of a shrine to the god Futsunushi no mikoto was requested by the Yoshida clan. The festival to the god is held on the twenty-third day of the sixth month." In modern times, the festival is held on the twenty-second of August, and includes a "Lion Dance" and parade. The street is purified with sand, and people sit alongside the road to greet the procession.

NOW ON AND UP the pass. Near the foot of the path, a sign reminds us,

ごみを見て山が泣く
When it sees trash, the mountain cries.

Hikers either heed or do not need the reminder, for the trail was completely free of any paper, plastic, or other refuse.

Five minutes in and I was winded. But it was a beautifully clear day, the temperature in about the mid-sixties, and here and there were sections of the old *ishitatami* laid in the early 1600s to secure human footing and horses' hooves. Along the path, hundreds of chestnuts lay scattered among the fallen leaves, mostly picked clean by the bears and wild pigs. They were pretty, but when I reached to admire one more closely, the sharp spines stabbed my hand. The wild animals clearly had more sense than I, and waited for them to open before they attempt to eat them. There was also some animal scat in two or three places, too small for bears, I told myself. Mr. Imai had earlier informed me that the forests were also inhabited by wild pigs, monkeys, and deer, so they might have been the culprits here.

A little more than a hundred yards up, there is a large pine called the *Toge no matsu*, the "Pine of the Pass." According to the *Kisoji junranki*, there was a song about this part of the slope, which is called *yatatezaka*. *Saka* means "slope," while *yatate* has a number of meanings: but the characters used—an arrow standing straight up—imply the very steep slope that it is.

松になりたや峠の松に上がり下りの客を待つ
Arriving at the pine!
at the Pine of the Pass,
waiting for the travelers
going up and down.[1]

Long ago, the Torii Pass—Torii Toge—was called either Yabuhara Toge or Narai Toge, depending on the traveler's destination. The people of Narai called it Yabuhara Toge while for the people of Yabuhara, it was the Narai Toge. There are a number of traditions concerning its current name—Torii Toge, or the Torii Gate Pass—but the most accepted one is related to a battle during the Warring States period (1482–1588). During this time, Kiso Yoshimoto was about to fight the forces of the Ogasawara clan. Climbing to the top of the pass, he did reverence to Mount Ontake, which loomed far in the distance, and prayed for victory in battle.

As the fight ensued, the victory was his, and he happily constructed a *torii* gate at the top of the pass. Ever since, it has been called the Torii Pass.

About halfway up the pass is the site of the *naka no chaya*—now just a small wooden structure much like a bus stop with a bench inside for taking a rest. According to the sign at the side of the *chaya*, it was here that an invading Takeda force of two thousand men was routed and defeated in February of 1583 by a much smaller army under the command of Kiso Yoshimasa. After a series of initial strategies and counterstrategies, the Takeda troops were caught in the deep snows of the pass and attacked from both above and below by the Kiso samurai. The Takeda lost over five hundred men that day, most of them buried in a swampy area nearby. As I read the sign, I was impressed that it states that the Takeda lost five hundred 名, or "names," rather than a simpler 人, or "person." This may be just common usage, but I imagined that this choice of words somehow gives those lost men some individuality and dignity. How anyone could fight on such a steep and narrow terrain is beyond me—and a whole army?

Finding that I had a few more ginger and black-sugar candies in my coat pocket, I finished them off with a prayer of thanks to my benefactor back in Niekawa, and, refreshed, I carried on.

By mid-morning I had gained the top of the pass and walked up to the *mine no chaya*, also called the *toge no chaya*. This is a clean wooden cabin with raised, wide wooden benches with room for about twenty people to sleep on inside, and a pleasant veranda with a view of the valley and mountains to the north along one edge on the outside. Around back are three very clean old-style Japanese toilets, indicating both respect for the mountain and that people often stop here. Next to the cabin, water gurgles from a rectangular wooden pipe into a large stone basin. In his *Ryoko yojinshu*, Yasumi Roan warned against drinking even clear running water, even in the mountains, and suggested mixing any water with a sort of Chinese medicine.[2] Pepper, he also noted, should be carried along to counter the bad mountain air and humidity. He adds,

> When anyone goes to an unknown part of the country, after a few days, the condition of their bowels may not be so good due to the change in water. You may feel heavy in the stomach, become constipated, break out in a rash or some eruption, or some other non-chronic ailment. And, though we say, "some other part of the country," surely we are under the same sky and breathe the same air, and should not be so concerned about the change in water. However, such is not the case. According to the natural features of the various parts of the country, and the differences in spring water, the temperatures, the weather, the character of the people, and even the local diets, are too numerous to count.
>
> If you take fish from mountain streams and put them in flatland ponds, for example, after a short while they will become disoriented and lose their bearings. Likewise, have a person live in an unfamiliar part of the country for two or three months, and he will become sick. You must be careful about this.

The water here looked awfully good, however, and I was thirsty enough to try it after the climb. After three refreshing and piercingly cold drafts from the ceramic bowl left on the stone basin, I signed the registry inside the cabin, reshouldered my pack, and moved on.

筧の水のあふるれば誰もひとくち
The water pipe overflowing,
a mouthful
for anyone.
—Santoka

The Kisoji turns off to the left about twenty or thirty yards from the *chaya,* and I soon entered a stand of huge chestnut trees. As I entered the dark shade of these trees, there was a *kumayoke*—a bell for scaring off bears—hanging at the side of the road, and I rang it twice, hoping that I was not just sounding a dinner bell for one of my large furry neighbors. These bells are hung on small wooden platforms about every fifty yards, and hikers are encouraged to take them seriously. A narrow satellite road meanders off to the left, and there is a stone monument marking Emperor Meiji's rest stop here in June of 1903. Strict precautions were taken to ensure the safety of such personages, and in all probability, the closest the emperor would have come to one of these animals would have been the hide he might have sat on in one of the three chayas that were here when he passed through. Nothing is left of the chayas, however, but a few unattended grave markers memorializing the men who maintained them. There are also a few stone pagodas, the oldest of which is dated 1711. When he passed through in 1803, Ota Nanpo noted that "at the stopping place with three *chaya*, they offer hides and gallbladders of bears."

The very top of the pass is nearly thirty-six hundred feet above sea level and is the watershed for the Kiso and Narai Rivers, which flow into the Pacific and the Sea of Japan, respectively. To the west, one can see Mount Ontake; to the south, Mount Komagatake. And at this point, on the right, there is an enormous chestnut tree, the *ko'umi no tochi,* or "Childbirth Chestnut," which is about nine feet in diameter. It is clearly old and quite rotted, and the main part of the trunk has a hole wide enough for a person to go inside. The story goes that, long ago, a beggar woman gave birth to a child here, and a man who had not been blessed with children found it abandoned inside the tree. The man took the child to his home in Yabuhara, and later it was discovered that if a woman boiled the nuts from this tree and drank the tea, she would soon become pregnant. Women reportedly followed this prescription—not only to become pregnant, but to guarantee an easy childbirth—well into the twentieth century. I considered gathering up a few of the chestnuts for friends back home but then, imagining the faces on the customs officials when I told them what I had, decided to leave them for another day.

In another fifty yards or so, I arrived at the small shrine built at the "Place for Worshipping Mount Ontake from Afar," in 1876. The steps to the shrine are guarded by a stone statue of Fudo Myo-o, whose angry visage encourages the visitor to use proper respect when entering the sacred grounds. When the writer of the *Kisoji no ki* climbed this road in 1709, he wrote down in his notes,

> The Torii Pass is even steeper than the Usui Pass. It is a dangerous place and difficult to ride a horse there. Long ago, there was a *torii* gate [at the top of the pass] dedicated to Mount Ontake, and thus the name, but there is no such *torii* gate there now.

A torii was rebuilt here in 1845, however, and then again in 1865.

This day, the steps up to the shrine had been roped off. Perhaps some of the stones had been upended by rains and erosion, and there was a sign on the rope that stated, "Danger—Do Not Enter." Nobody was around, and I was tempted to climb over the ropes but decided to honor the gods from the bottom of the steps. The scowling face on the statue of Fudo Myo-o behind me stated clearly that it was the right thing to do. It had been a long way to come for this, and it was a beautiful clear day to view Mount Ontake from the shrine. Not a bad omen, I hoped.

Continuing on and now descending the path, in about fifty yards I found that a new temporary trail had been opened up to the spot behind the shrine to view and worship Mount Ontake. It was quite steep, but I took heart and was rewarded at the top with a fine view of Mount Ontake, pale blue in the distance and still clear of snow, and a walk around the *jinja*. Large, scary old statues of Fudo, Marishiten, and other gods and long-ago priests connected with Mount Ontake are clustered around the area and add to the atmosphere of mountain religion and gods of whom we are only vaguely aware. It was cold here at the top of the pass, and I felt an uneasy chill. Going around to the front of the empty shrine, I clapped my hands twice to show my respect, dropped twenty yen into the offering box through a small window, and carried on downhill again.

At the bottom of this new temporary path, there is a narrow, level area called Maruyama Park, equipped with two wooden benches on which hikers might rest a while. There are also two stone monuments, each engraved with a haiku by Basho.

> 木曽の栃 うき世の人の土産かな
> Horse chestnuts of the Kiso
> souvenirs for those
> of this floating world.

> 雲雀よりうへにやすらふ嶺かな
> Soaring above
> the skylark:
> the mountain peak!

In this same area is a small spring still issuing pure water called *yoshinaka tsuzuri mizu*, or "Water for Yoshinaka's Inkstone." Tradition has it that when Yoshinaka rebelled against the Heike and was advancing to Kyoto to subdue them, he took water from this spring to write an offering to Mount Ontake in supplication for victory. A corner of the park overlooks the Kiso River and the post town of Yabuhara, and I could imagine how congested this very spot must have been during the Edo period, as the retinues of daimyo and crowds of commoners waited for those ahead of them to surmount the narrow and steep trail on their way to Narai.

Halfway down the hill was another kumayoke bell, which, again, I rang enthusiastically. The pass seemed to be quite alive with bears and statues of Fudo Myo-o, and I was reminded of the poet Gary Snyder's conflation of the two in his "Smokey the Bear

Sutra," both bear and Buddhist avatar representing the preservation of the wild and an undisturbed mind. As an extra precaution, I chanted Fudo Myo-o's mantra with each ring of the bell.

> Nama samanta vajranam
> chanda maharoshana spataya
> hum traka ham nam.

This Buddhist mantra is recited to remove the scary bears of our own minds, not the ones we may encounter in the wild, but it still seemed appropriate.

A little past the bell, the path once again became ishitatami, alongside of which was a low stone wall, the ancient stones completely covered with moss. Gradually, I entered a neighborhood of Yabuhara, but the path did not get any less precipitous. In 1937, the writer of the *Kiso kotsushi* wrote,

> As you descend the Torii Pass, while the descent is such that a mortar could not be placed upright, people's houses are already lining the steep road on both sides. On the sliding doors erected out in front are posted signs advertising meals of a single bowl of rice or rice mixed with chestnuts. There are also paper signboards written in bold strokes advertising the combs that are such famous products for the area. The Torii Pass is at the back of this place, and the Kiso River can be seen below. Yabuhara is on the left and the distant Ogiso Valley on the right, and here is a single building above a precipice, the well-known *takasho yakusho*.

Alas, the signs advertising bowls of rice and chestnuts are gone, and the site of the once-important *takasho yakusho,* called "Hawk Castle" by the villagers, is now just a small gravelly lot, a corner of which was today occupied by someone's automobile. The view of the autumnal mountains and Kiso River was just as beautiful, though, and I found it a lovely spot to just stand and catch my breath.

During the Edo period, the *takasho yakusho* was the residence of the hawk-nesting official, who would come once a year when the hawk fledglings were hatched in the Kiso. This official, called the "Nest Master," inspected the nests and the fledglings that the commoners were able to find for him and collected a considerable reward for every three or four of the baby birds he was able to acquire and take care of. Although hawking was popular among many of the feudal lords, the Kiso was heavily controlled by the Owari fief, which no doubt cornered a profitable market for prospective buyers until at least 1872.

After a short rest at the site of the former Hawk Castle, I walked down the last of the steep incline and, the once-dreaded Torii Pass behind me, was finally on the main road of the post town of Yabuhara.

COURSE TIME
Narai-shuku to Yabuhara-shuku: 5 kilometers (3 miles). 3 hours, 15 minutes.

6 Yabuhara ELEVATION 2,775 FEET

When you enter the post town of Yabuhara, the atmosphere is one of wealth and prosperity. There are many things for sale, such as the o-roku *combs and the chopsticks made of Japanese yew, and these products are seen in every province. Tonight I am staying at the house of a certain Mr. Komeya. The master is an honest and sincere man, and told me a number of stories. I asked him about the* o-roku *combs, and he told me there was once a woman by the name of O-roku who made the combs from the* minebari *tree.*[1]

—Ota Nanpo, 1802

THE STORY of the *o-roku* combs, which are for sale in many Yabuhara shops, goes something like this:

During the Genroku era (1688–1705), there was a woman working at a certain inn in Tsumago by the name of O-roku. O-roku was troubled by headaches, but one night the god of Mount Ontake appeared to her in a dream and said that she would be cured by wearing a *minebari* comb in her hair. She became extremely talented in making these combs, and as a result of various efforts, invented the fine-toothed comb we use nowadays. Offering them for sale to the travelers who stayed the night at the inn, she won high acclaim and a good reputation. Because Tsumago was a post town on the Kiso Road, the people who purchased them gradually increased, and the people in the post town eventually imitated her and made their own combs. Gradually, production increased, but the kind of tree used for the comb material became scarce, and

67

was sought in the upper reaches of the Kiso Valley near the Torii Pass. A wealth of raw material was carried off to Tsumago right before the eyes of the people of Yabuhara, but no matter how they tried, they could not create the same combs themselves. Finally, a certain Sanjuya disguised himself as a mendicant Zen priest of the Fuke sect, and, wearing a hood and playing the *shakuhachi,* went to Tsumago, acquired the comb-making technique, and returned to Yabuhara. For the good of the community, he then passed on the secret, the work of fine-toothed comb production spread throughout Yabuhara, which in the end wrested the market from Tsumago.

—From *Kiso: Rekishi to minzoku wo tazunete*

As I walked south through the town, I passed the Komeya, where I had spent a night a number of years ago. The old sign in front of the shop advertising the name of an Edo-period proprietor, Komeya Yosaemon—perhaps the one mentioned by Ota Nanpo—was still there. The inn was now closed, however, as the man who had provided me with such hospitality, good meals, and good stories passed away in 2012. The building is an historic one and will remain untouched, but his son had earlier informed me by phone that no one in the family wants to carry on the work of taking care of an old inn.

Although it was still before noon, the climb over the Torii Pass had worked on my appetite, and I searched out the Shimizu-ya, a small shop accoutered with five huge cedar-slab tables, where my wife, Emily, and I had dined some fifteen years before as we passed through. Despite the early hour, I was kindly let in by the elderly husband and wife, who welcomed me with happy smiles. I ordered an *unagi-don,* barbecued eel on a bowl of rice, with a bottle of nonalcoholic beer, and sat down at one of the tables that had been cut horizontally from the trunk of the tree to preserve its natural shape.

When the meal arrived, I could see that the unagi was very, very fresh and was reminded of the Buddha's injunction against "eating meat that was killed just for you." I felt regret but eagerly finished everything in the bowl, polished off the "beer," and hoped that I could be a better person. As I paid my bill, old Mr. Shimizu brought me an *o-miyage*, a souvenir, a cedar coaster with eighty tree rings, on which he had printed his own *hanga*—a depiction of two horses, the date, and a poem. He made them himself, he said and, looking at my backpack, added that he hoped it would not become extra luggage.

Back out on to the street, I continued walking south and looked for my night's lodging, the Isami-ya. Yabuhara looks much like any small Japanese mountain village but still retains a few old houses with overhanging balconies and latticed doorways. There is running water at the corner of almost every street, flowing from wooden spigots into large wooden basins, with dippers from which anyone may take a drink. The poet Santoka loved water, as much if not more than sake, and passed through Yabuhara at least three times on his unending journeys. The poem he perhaps wrote here reads,

> へうへうとして水を味わう
> Tasting the water,
> my heart
> afloat.

On this day, all of the comb shops were closed because of a folk-craft festival in Narai, but I passed one, the Miyakawa Shiryokan, which I remembered well from years ago. I had been talking to the young proprietor, when he showed me some cards hand-written by the poets Buson and Basho, the latter traveling the Kiso Road in 1685 and 1688, stopping in Yabuhara both times. Yamaoka Tesshu had also passed through during the early Meiji period and left a piece of his unique calligraphy as well. The shop had operated as an inn during the Edo and Meiji periods, and when poor but famous poets stayed, they would write their poems on *tansaku*—rectangular cuts of stiff paper—and leave them instead of paying the usual fare. When I asked the proprietor what generation of the family he was, his response was, "Well, you know, people here in Yabuhara still think of us as newcomers because we originally came from a few valleys over from here about three hundred years ago. I'm just the ninth generation running this shop."

Mr. Miyagawa's family is actually descended from warriors who served their lords during the Namboku period (1336–92) but for the last 170 years or so had been doctors who were allowed to carry swords because of their status.

Like other towns on the Kiso, Yabuhara has experienced its own ups and downs. When Okada Zenkuro made his inspection tour in 1839, he made this sympathetic report:

> This post town lies at the highest elevation in the valley that is the source of the Kiso River, so the cold is extreme during the winter and spring. Agriculture is carried out only in vegetable fields bordered by low stone walls, and making a living in this way is difficult. Thus, since ancient times, the people have turned to making combs of wood and fine utensils out of Japanese cypress. Some years ago, such goods brought excellent prices, and grains were at a low price, so a good living was made by such work, and the local population increased. Because of this, the business of going and coming in the post town went well, and similar work was started by many people throughout the provinces. Sooner or later, the prices of such items fell, profits decreased, and the price of grains increased. With the poor harvests of 1837, it was difficult to make profit enough for food provisions, and gradually people were at such extremities that they could not sell their clothing, household goods, the tools of their trades, or even their rice and vegetable fields. The result was that many people starved to death or left the area, the number of houses decreased, and the post town went into debt.

The post town, however, rebounded and, with the number of people traveling the Nakasendo in the remaining part of the century and their demand for lodging and souvenirs, flourished once again.

Walking on, I finally found my inn close to the southern end of the town, but the o-kami-san was out, and no one responded to my calls at the entranceway.

Backtracking, I checked my backpack at the train station, walked back along the main street, and then climbed the hill in back of the town up to the Gokurakuji, a Zen Buddhist temple founded in 1571. Entering through the huge front gate, the traveler is struck by the massive size of this wooden temple, which is fronted by a large gravel foreyard with statues of Kannon, Jizo, and other bodhisattvas placed here and there. Unfortunately, the temple, too, was closed due to the festival in Narai, and I sat down on a low stone wall to rest.

There is an exquisite garden to the rear of this temple, which had been created in the style of the famous Kobori Enshu (1579–1647), a master of Japanese art, poetry, tea ceremony, and gardening. While walking through the grounds over a decade ago, I learned that the garden had not one, but two master gardeners—one for the garden in general and one who specializes in pines. In the center of the garden, there is a single vertical rock, around which the rest of the stones, bushes, and trees are asymmetrically arranged. There is also a large boat-shaped rock, the *takarabune*—the ship transporting the "Seven Happy Gods"—with a pine shaped like a standing crane growing in its center. The temple also houses paintings by Sesshu and the Zen priests Hakuin and Takuan; and on the left side of the main hall is a shrine for O-roku, where a comb memorial service is held every September 4.

It was a beautiful sunny day with a cloudless sky, and my stomach was full, so I decided to take a slow walk back through the Yabuhara Jinja, a large wooded shrine next to the Gokurakuji. Along with the dark cypress and cedar trees, the shrine was spotted here and there with fall flowers I could not identify, enough so that it was as much an arboretum as a holy place. Although the main hall was built only in 1827, the shrine itself was founded in 680 and is dedicated to the avatar of Kumano Jinja (bears again, Kumano meaning "Bear Field"), extant since 81 B.C.E.

To give the o-kami-san of my inn more time to do her chores, I descended the hill and headed back north to the Ogino-ya, where I was welcomed by the proprietor, Mr. Jinmura, and a young waitress. This shop specializes in soba, or buckwheat noodles, and has the feel of an Edo-period establishment. The ceiling is perhaps two stories high, with rafters of dark wood blackened from years of smoke that rose up from the central hearth. All around this ash-filled hearth—about ten feet long and four feet wide—is a wooden deck that functions as a table, its surface also smooth and dark from years of use. A large iron kettle hangs over the hearth and emits steam heated by the charcoal below. High windows allow in an opaque light, which seems to focus on two wall-mounted *kamidanas,* or "god shelves"—one dedicated to the gods of Mount Ontake, the other to Mr. Jinmura's ancestors. I ordered a *tokkuri* of cold sake, which was delivered on a wooden tray in a tall, unglazed open *kyusu* and a cup in the same style. While feeling just a little guilty for such an early indulgence, I was encouraged by this poem quoted in the *Ryoko yojinshu:*

> 上戸ても旅て大酒はすべからす折々すこしのめはりやうやく
>
> As for drinking
> when on a journey,
> do not drink too much.
> Yet just a little from time to time
> is good medicine.

And Kaibara Ekiken, who no doubt stopped here to sample the local wares, wrote in the *Yojokun,* his notes on health, "Sake is the nectar of Heaven. If you drink just a little, it reinforces your yang *ch'i,* softens youthful vigor, circulates respiration, drives away depression, stimulates interest in the world, and is greatly beneficial to man." A wood-burning stove next to me provided some additional heat.

As I settled in to my sake, which was a *tokubetsu junmai* and one of the best I'd ever tasted, Mr. Jinmura and his waitress served a group of four of five people who had just come in, and then came over to chat. He is an enthusiastic and cheerful man of about fifty, and explained to me that, although his family originally came Miya no koshi, the next post town, they had been at this location for some 680 years. He went on to say that before this place became a soba shop, it was a sort of convenience store (a *konbini*, in his words), or to use a more proper Japanese word, a *zakkaya*, selling various goods to people who passed by in front on the Kiso Road. A fire destroyed everything 130 years ago, but the main building and storehouse were restored after that. Many years ago, he said, it was a huge shop, with numerous employees busy at work as the feudal lord processions on their way to Edo and back passed by right in front. Yabuhara was the largest town in the Kiso at that time—which means it was the largest in frontage along the road—and so taxed heavily.

Soon, the other customers joined in the conversation, and we were informed that both the poet Santoka and the eccentric potter/chef Rosanjin had stopped by this shop in the past. After an hour of friendly talk, the other customers and I took our leave, Mr. Jinmura and his waitress bowed us out on their knees, and we were all in good spirits.

Just across the street from the Ogino-ya is the Yugawa sake distillery, with a magnificent *sakabayashi* (ball of cedar leaves and twigs, signifying a sake establishment) hanging over the entranceway. Established in the early Edo period, it is now well over three hundred years old and still producing a fine sake called—what else?—Kisoji (or, The Kiso Road). In 1975, the proprietor was the fourteenth-generation brewery master, operating the highest-elevation distillery in Japan. Some years ago, I had been given a tour of this brewery and walked through the warehouses full of shiny steel vats of a fermenting sort of soup. You start with rice, my guide explained, clean it with the pure water of the Kiso, steam it to the consistency of *gohan*—the rice you eat in Japanese restaurants—cool it, and then put it into the vats. The yeast is prepared elsewhere and then added. Traditionally for local sakes, as the fermenting semiliquid glop was stirred with large paddles by hand, there was a song sung at each stage, limiting exactly the time it was to be attended to. If the stirring was finished before or after the song, the mixture would not be right. Looking at the mechanized production here, I had wondered if the old songs were still remembered by even the oldest of the workers, who were now dressed in clean uniforms and wore hardhats. It was now all down to a computerized science, but my cups of the *tokubetsu junmai* at the Ogino-ya had spoken quite eloquently of its continued high level of quality.

I now once again headed south, collected my backpack from the railroad station, and found that the o-kami-san of my inn, a pleasant woman of about fifty, had returned. She was happy to show me up to my room, which was on the second floor, overlooking the train station a hundred or so yards away. The station itself is not very big and, as train stations do, emotes a feeling of travel, transience, and an odd sense of nostalgia for something of which you have no clear memory. I opened up the windows to get a better view, checked out the map for tomorrow, and took a break. My calves and thighs had been sore the day before, and they were now again. More ominously, there seemed to be some very large blisters forming on my feet. Going over the pass, I had ascended about 750 feet and descended about 825. As I closed my eyes, I noticed that my ceiling had been very tastefully constructed with cedar planking and cherrywood rafters. There was a faint scent of incense coming from the first floor, and I let go and went to sleep.

Later, there was a dinner downstairs of trout, hamburger, mashed potatoes, egg soup, three or four different country vegetables,

---

---

chikuwa, rice, and Japanese tea. I did my best and waddled back to my room, wondering if the o-kami-san thought I hadn't eaten in a week. There is a washing machine and dryer in the Isami-ya, so after washing my clothes, I took a long soaking bath. Clothes dried, folded, and put back into my backpack, I finally stretched out on my futon, watched a television program on Japanese birds, and then read a little more Confucius. Sure enough, he always has something appropriate.

君子食無求飽

In dining, the Gentleman does not seek satiety.

Unable to keep my eyes open, I turned out the light to sounds of the last train pulling out of the station.

COURSE TIME
Yabuhara-shuku to Miya no koshi-shuku: 8 kilometers (4.8 miles).
3 hours, 20 minutes.

7 Miya no koshi ELEVATION 2,670 FEET

The bell of the Gion Temple echoes the transience of all things. The hue of the flowers of the sala tree gives warning that whoever rises will surely fall. The prideful will not last long, just like the dream on a night of spring. The bold and dauntless man will also, in the end, come to ruin, exactly like the dust before the wind.

—*Heike monogatari*, Book 1

THE WHISTLE of the 6:21 local train invited me to join the day, so I folded up my futon, packed everything but my toothbrush, and headed downstairs for a breakfast of poached salmon, yogurt, one fried egg in a small pot, miso soup, *natto,* rice, pickles, and Japanese tea—fuel for the day.

It was a cloudy, cold day, mists were moving between the mountains, and I was happy to find a vending machine right outside the entrance to the inn. Purchasing two cans of my favorite Japanese coffee—Boss café au lait—I slowly sipped down one (they are hot) and put the other in my coat pocket as a hand warmer. The o-kami-san was still bowing me off as I turned the corner onto the national highway with its trucks and cars, but the Kiso River was rushing and gurgling over river rocks below me on my right, and ahead were mountains folding into mountains, covered in reds, yellows, purples, and greens. In a short while, the Nakasendo turned away from the highway, and the path entered a dark cedar forest punctuated by streams flowing down the mountain and into the river, now on my left. With the traffic gone, the sound of water

77

was everywhere. With his two small rattan suitcases hung over his chest and back, the shabby old loner Santoka would have traveled along this same road some eighty years ago. Two of his free haiku:

たたずめば水音のはてもなし
Pausing a moment,
the sound of rivers and streams
without end.

水音のとほくちかくなりて道は
The road:
the sound of water
near and far.

The road now led through a tiny hamlet of houses and then wound through an open area of rice fields that had already been harvested, the clumps of cut stalks neatly dotting the dry ground. The Chuo-sen railroad crosses the Nakasendo here; the barrier came down, and the lights flashed on and off. I stopped and waved my hat as the train whizzed by, but the passengers were busy reading their newspapers and magazines, and only one little girl waved happily back from the coach window.

Soon I was back on the national highway, and in less than a quarter mile, it entered the Yamabuki Tunnel. Years ago, I walked with my wife and two of our friends through this long and dark tunnel on its very narrow sidewalks, small thin towels given to us by our inns as souvenirs wrapped around our noses and mouths. It was scarier than any of us cared to admit to each other until later that night over sake and dinner, and I did not relish walking through it again. Luck was with me this time, however, and I spied an old road on the other side of the highway that we had not seen before, and what looked like a wooden guidepost on which was clearly carved, "Miya no koshi, 2 km." I scampered across the highway and found that this better route was an old narrow road, now closed to cars and open only to hikers. The Kiso River was on my left once again, the mountains very close in, and fall colors everywhere. One tree in particular stood out from the others, full of bright yellow leaves stretching almost all the way across the river. The place was lonely and very quiet, with weeds and small trees poking up through the cracked asphalt. Once again the only sound was that of the clear blue-green water rushing and jumping over rocks and boulders of all sizes.

水はみんな滝となり秋ふかし

All the streams
becoming waterfalls:
deep autumn.
—Santoka

此道や行人なしに秋の暮

On this road
no one goes:
dusk in autumn
—Basho

A little farther along, and I entered the hamlet of Hiyoshi, on the right of which is Mount Yamabuki. This is said to have been the residence of Lady Yamabuki, about whom the *Kisoji meisho zue* states:

> In the *Heike monogatari* it says that Yoshinaka had two concubines; one was Tomoe, the other Yamabuki. During the battle of Genryaku, Yamabuki fell ill, and stayed with a doctor in the capital. However, in the *Genpei suisaki*, we are told that Yoshinaka's two concubines were Tomoe and Aoi. Both were great warriors, but Aoi was killed in the battle at Mount Tonami. These two stories are not the same, and some say that Yamabuki was the wife of Saito Betto Sanemori. We still do not know the truth.

Whoever this Yamabuki was, the entire Kiso Valley, and especially this area, is imbued with the memory of Kiso Yoshinaka, his mistresses, and his descendants.

Born in 1154 in the northeastern province of Musashi, Yoshinaka was a member of a branch of the Minamoto clan, one of the two clans fighting for hegemony during the twelfth century. His father was killed in internecine warfare when Yoshinaka was only one year old, and he was taken to the Kiso to be raised by a powerful relative. Yoshinaka prospered in the Kiso, building a mansion in Miya no koshi, and commanded several thousand soldiers. In 1180, he felt his opportunity had come, raised the flag of rebellion against the Taira—the other great clan at the time—and marched to Kyoto, then controlled by Taira Kiyomori. Within two years, the Taira were defeated and Yoshinaka was the first to enter the capital, where he was greeted as a hero. Political intrigue coupled with what many in the refined and cultured capital, Kyoto, considered to be the boorishness, arrogance, and countrified ways of Yoshinaka and his samurai, however, eventually led to his ouster and death in a battle with the troops of his cousin, Yoritomo. Yoshinaka had been called the Asahi Shogun, or "Sunrise Shogun," and was only thirty-one years old when he died.

Continuing on around Mount Yamabuki, I encountered an elderly man with a paralyzed right arm clearing rocks away from a small stone moment engraved with a poem. Without much prompting, he chanted the verse to me but mumbled so badly I could only make out the words "Kiso" and maybe "Yoshinaka." With a large smile, he informed me that he had written the poem himself, and then devotedly got back to work. The picked flowers at his side would no doubt soon adorn his little memorial. Yoshinaka has been dead for over nine hundred years but lives on here, even in this old man's dreams.

Yoshinaka's other concubine—said to be his favorite—was Tomoe Gozen, also from Miya no koshi according to legend. In the thirteenth-century work *Heike monogatari*, we read that

Tomoe had a fair complexion and long hair, and her face was truly beautiful. She was uncommonly skillful with a bow, and was a spirited warrior when mounted on a horse. Even when on foot, when she held a sword, even the gods and demons would not approach her. She was a match for a thousand men.

Tomoe survived the battle where Yoshinaka died, but not before taking one or two more heads. She then escaped and, perhaps, became a Buddhist nun in one of the northern provinces.

After a few minutes' walk, I arrived at the *tomoe ga fuchi,* where a tiny trickle of a waterfall enters a broad pond fed by a stream where Tomoe is said to have turned into a dragon as the water's guardian spirit. It is a quiet place with a small pavilion where travelers can take off their backpacks and rest for a while. Attached to a pillar of the pavilion was a rain-spotted notebook registry for guests to sign. I added my signature but declined to try my hand at a poem inspired by the beauty of the area, which other visitors had done with varying degrees of success. There was, however, a stone monument engraved with a haiku next to the bridge that crosses the stream, and the poet was a professional, Kyoroku, who lived during the Edo period.

山吹も巴もいでて田植かな
The mountain roses, and
Tomoe, too, come out:
planting the rice.

Yamabuki 山吹, the name of his other concubine, means "mountain rose." *Tomoe* 巴 means a "whirl" or "eddy," much as might be seen here at the waterfall and pond. Two tomoe together indicate two large commas united to make a perfect circle, perhaps a metaphor for Yoshinaka's feelings about his concubines.

My route now became a series of uphill winding roads, as I looked for the famous Hata-age Hachiman Shrine where Yoshinaka had actually raised the flag of rebellion in this faraway place.

There were few signs to go by, and when I did find it, I was still not so sure that I had. The shrine, where once a thousand men raised their swords and spears, is very small, about the size of a private teahouse. At its side is the trunk of a once-giant zelkova tree—now either mostly lightning struck or rotted, but still luxuriant with leaves—which appears to have been there since the time of Yoshinaka. Nothing else remains. His extensive mansion is said to have been next to the shrine, but now there are only dry rice fields, some white plastic-covered greenhouses, and a few recently planted pines. The atmosphere is one of *mujo*, or "impermanence," the theme of not only the *Heike monogatari,* but a good part of Japanese classical literature. From the wooden bench where I sat, the Kiso Valley and the town of Miya no koshi were visible below, while the national highway rumbled on in the distance.

Of Miya no koshi, the *Shokoku dochu tabikagami* of 1847 states only that "in this area, houses made only of wooden planks are more prevalent than in Yabuhara, and there is no bamboo. This is a bad mountain district." A few years before, Okada Zenkuro had noted,

> The mountains are low in this post town, so there are places that could be opened for rice and vegetable fields. But it is still at a high elevation and intensely cold, so there are few fields, the harvests are meager, and it is difficult to make a living by agriculture. Moreover, the commercial roads to the more prosperous areas east and west are somewhat far and transportation fees are numerous and high-priced, and salt and similar items are expensive. Thus, it is difficult to make a living, and many people are in debt. . . . In years past, people raised oxen and made a living from the fees paid for transporting goods from Nagoya, Fukushima, Ina and Matsumoto. Recently, however, conditions have worsened, and the number of oxen has been greatly reduced.

At one time, this was a post town for the relay of post horses, with one honjin, one waki-honjin, and a line of twenty-one inns. Today, however, every one of those inns is gone, the last having been run by a wonderful old lady, Mrs. Kato, whose warm hospitality I received with my wife and friends a number of times. When she passed away a few years ago, her daughter kept the inn as a residence, where she now brings up her family, but she herself commutes every day to a job in Kiso Fukushima. The house is next door to the old honjin, now abandoned and overgrown with vegetation, but one imagines that Mrs. Kato's ancestors must have had a lively business when the town was thriving.

The Kiso River runs through the middle of Miya no koshi and is spanned by several bridges before winding off to the west. A short walk from the red Temple Bridge is the Toku'onji, a Buddhist temple founded in 1169 but moved to its present location in 1776. It is a small but well-kept temple, and its copper roof was artfully replaced some years ago. While serving one of her incomparable dinners one night, Mrs. Kato remarked that each of the parishioners had had to help pay for this renovation, each according to his or her level of membership. Mrs. Kato's contribution, she said with a grimace, was three hundred thousand yen—equivalent to more than three thousand dollars at the time—a hefty bill for an elderly woman running an inn. The temple nowadays is famous for containing the mortuary tablet of Yoshinaka (and now, no doubt, Mrs. Kato's, as well) and is the place where visitors pray for the enlightenment of his soul. To the left of the main hall is a wooden sculpture of Yoshinaka, and behind this is his grave marker, covered with moss beneath a tree, and those of Tomoe and Yoshinaka's mother.

I left a prayer for all of them, dropped a hundred-yen coin in the offering box, and moved on, passing the Yoshinaka Museum on my way back to the Nakasendo, at this juncture the unimposing narrow main street of town.

Except for the Toku'onji and the Yoshinaka Museum, Miya no koshi (literally, "at the hip of the shrine") is yet another quiet mountain village—a barber shop, one grocery store, and an elementary and middle school for the entire area. Its prosaic appearance, however, hides a long and complicated history. Earthenware pottery, porcelain objects, bronze implements, and eight-cornered bronze mirrors dating from the Jomon to the Heian and Kamakura periods have been unearthed along the bank of the river, and these, along with the artifacts and illustrations of Yoshinaka's time, are displayed in the museum. Records show that there were large residences and even iron foundries in the surrounding area, indicating that this had once been an important source for raw materials since the earliest times—a place of mansions and commerce. But for whatever reason—the kids grow up, move to the big city, and don't come back, or there are not enough visitors to support an inn—there are no more lodgings for travelers in Miya no koshi.

The *Hojoki,* the thirteenth-century essay by the priest Kamo no Chomei, laments,

> The current of the moving river is unending, but the water is never the same. The bubbles floating on the surface, now come together, now dissolve, and there is not an example of them lasting for long. In this world, men and their houses are just like this. . . . Both battle with impermanence, but they are no different than the dew on the morning glory. The dew will fall and the flower remains, but though we say "remains," it wilts in the morning sun. Or, the flower will fade and the dew not vanish, but though we say "not vanish," it does not wait the close of day.

I struck out for the next village, Harano. The sky was beginning to darken, and I was acutely aware that my feet were not as comfortable as they should have been; but my destination—by the map—was not too far away. Nevertheless, I quickened my steps, hoping to outpace the coming rain.

About four hundred yards past the outskirts of Miya no koshi, in the neighborhood of Shinoshima, there is a deep pool on the opposite bank of the Kiso River, which the local people call the *jakiri no fuchi,* or the "Killing the Snake Pond." According to the *Kisoji meisho zue,*

Everyone says that a long time ago there was a farmer who was cutting grass along this bank. It was tough work, so he got tired and lay down on the bank to take a nap. Suddenly, he smelled something terrible, jumped up in surprise, and saw that a huge serpent had come up and opened its mouth wide to swallow him. At that moment, he swung his sickle and cut the serpent down. The serpent floated in the water, turning over and over, and finally died. For this reason, the pool is called "Killing the Snake Pond." The farmer put away his sickle and passed it on to his descendants. If anyone gets sick with the ague, he will recover immediately just by looking at this sickle.

Quiet pools and poisonous snakes often appear in old Japanese tales, which, often enough, do not end as happily as this one.

At the tiny unoccupied Shinoshima railroad station, I sat down on a convenient rock and looked across the river to where the pool should have been. It was a lonely little spot, just the right place to encounter a large snake, but it was just beginning to sprinkle, so I decided to move on.

The Nakasendo now continued up a steady incline, at the top of which was a splendid view of the Komagatake Sanmyaku, an extended mountain range to the southeast. According to the *Kisoji anken zue,*

At the top of Mount Komagatake, there is a huge boulder that resembles a colt [*koma*], hence the name, Komagatake, or Colt Peak. This is a high mountain; the snows melt in the sixth month, but begin accumulating again in the eighth.

My friend Ichikawa Takashi hiked with me up that mountain in July of 1969. I remember it being cold enough then, and stopping to drink from the streams running down from the peaks was like putting my lips to ice.

This was a long walk, but someone had been thoughtful enough to plant thick rows of orange and red nasturtiums along the road-side—a pleasant distraction from painful feet. Eventually the view was shut off by a dark cedar forest on the east, and the Kiso River flowed away to the west, out of earshot but not of sight. Shortly before the outskirts of Harano, there is leveled-out ground up against a small hill occupied by a number of stone monuments and some five- or six-foot stone statues, some of which are likely connected with Mount Ontake, but I could not be sure.

Most interesting to me was one I often encountered by the roadside in the Kiso, a two- or three-foot stone monument engraved with the Chinese characters 庚申 (*koshin*). In the past, I had asked local people what the characters meant, but no one had come up with a satisfactory answer, and some just shrugged their shoulders as if to say, "Who knows?" Finally, I looked it up in my Chinese-Japanese dictionary and found this explanation: According to an ancient Taoist tradition imported to Japan, there are three worms called the *sanshichu* that live in our stomachs. On a certain night of the year—indicated by the calendrical term *koshin*, or *kanoesaru*—the worms travel up to heaven while the person is sleeping and inform the Yellow Emperor of all his or her bad deeds. To prevent this uncomfortable and embarrassing situation, people will stay up all night celebrating the gods and buddhas, no doubt accompanied by plenty of singing and drinking, and perhaps a few more bad deeds, to boot. Interestingly, this belief is somehow related to the three monkeys of "See no evil, speak no evil, and hear no evil," perhaps because 申, *shin,* is an old zodiac character for monkey and is also pronounced *saru,* "monkey" in Japanese.

Finally, the road leads into old Harano, an *ai no shuku,* or in-between post town. There are still some old wooden homes built in what is called the "extended beam style," and just a little farther ahead stands a signpost indicating the exact center of the Nakasendo. The traditional homes soon give way to more modern structures, however, and the national highway can be seen and heard up to the east. Okada Zenkuro found this to be a place of fertile fields and a number of rice paddies, and also noted that members of the Kiso clan had lived here for many generations.

Still, he could see that the town was "under the shadow" of Mount Komagatake, so the weather is quite cold and the harvested crops inferior to other places.

Today, thanks to the national highway, the old resting station is quite prosperous. As I walked through a new neighborhood, I asked for directions to my inn. It was not right on the Nakasendo, I was told, and was instructed to take a left turn, cross over the national highway, and climb up the hill to the Komao (the "Colt King"), Yoshinaka's childhood name and that of my lodging for the night. Taking the turn left, I crossed a covered culvert and noticed a small stone monument engraved with 水神, "water god," still revered though running underground and next to a well-traveled road. The natural elements of life are not ignored here, though unseen and passed quickly by.

The drizzle began in earnest as I crossed the national highway—heavy traffic of trucks and cars—and the climb up was again steeper than I would have liked. And, although I asked several times about the Komao, the answer was always the same: "Just another ten minutes." At last, after passing a roadside market and restaurant and—surprisingly in this largely Buddhist country—a Kingdom Hall of the Jehovah's Witnesses, I found a large three-story modern building, with an expansive but minimalist garden, a circular driveway, and small buses full of middle-aged men and women being dropped off and picked up. This was the Komao—not a ryokan or minshuku at all, but a hot spring destination for tourists.

This was not exactly a welcome surprise—I prefer traditional inns—but I had made my reservations sight unseen, and I was wet and tired and ready to stop for a while. Despite my bedraggled appearance, the concierge greeted me with a happy smile and showed me to my second-floor room, the Niekawa, which was quite traditional—tatami, a low table, and copies of Hiroshige's prints of the Kiso Road on the wall. There was also a television and a small porch with a writing table and chair. Purchasing an Asahi beer from the hallway vending machine, I settled in and tried to dry myself out; outside, the rain was coming down hard (or *zaa zaa,* as they say in Japanese).

Eventually I realized that I had not eaten since breakfast at the Isami-ya. Food is not served at the Komao until six in the evening, so I grabbed my miniscule umbrella, put on my wet boots, and headed out. The rain had let up a little, although the streams on both sides of the road were now full and rushing their way down the hill toward the Kiso. After a meal of a hot bowl of tempura udon and a vending machine "cappuccino" at a sort of truck stop/ vegetable stand/restaurant, I wandered next door to a small bookstore, and I was delighted to find three slim volumes on local folktales, collected by local high school students. One of these books contained a version of the above-mentioned Killing the Snake Pond, and I anticipated that they would make for fun reading after the serious Confucius.

Putting my new treasures into a plastic bag, the store manager kindly walked out into the rain with me and directed me to the Rinshoji, formerly a Tendai sect temple but now under the auspices of Rinzai Zen. This temple was built in 1169 and was the family temple of Nakahara Kaneto, Yoshinaka's foster father. Kaneto shaved his head and entered religion when Yoshinaka left for the capital, so he may have sensed the coming disaster. His grave marker is one of the many at the foot of the mountain.

It was a short hike, but the sidewalk along the national highway seemed dangerously narrow and close to the trucks flying by, and I was soaked again by the time I reached the temple. Once inside the main gate, six stone statues of Jizo greeted me as I entered, and facing the temple itself was a mid-sized garden with low pines, a small pond with two or three koi, and artificial hills. The noisy speed of the highway was suddenly inaudible, or at least I was not aware of it.

Taking heart, I took off my wet boots, walked up the wooden temple steps, and rang the small, round doorbell. Sure enough, the priest's wife opened the sliding door with a smile and asked me what she could do for me. I explained that I was hiking along the Kiso Road and was interested in the cultural places along the way. She graciously showed me in, and I was once again struck as to how wealthy the Kiso Valley must have been at one time—no doubt due to its place on the Nakasendo and its role as a business route and a road for pilgrims. This temple is not particularly large but is extremely ornate, with elaborate gold-plated fixtures hanging from the ceiling and an extraordinarily embellished altar, centered in front of a gold-plated image of Kannon. The many cushions inside the hallway indicated that there is a good-sized congregation here.

Over Japanese tea and rice cakes, the priest's wife explained that Zen temples are not always the sites of the long meditation periods and strict austerities that we imagine in the West. There are such temples, and on the Kiso Road as well, but the temples in the towns are largely supported by parishioners, whose families were required by the central government to register with one temple or another as far back as the Edo period. This parish system continues on today, and Mrs. Kato's three-hundred-thousand-yen contribution to her temple's repairs is a case in point. Nowadays, as three hundred years ago, the parishioners will gather at the temple for special celebratory days, funerals, or weekend sermons. The priest must also visit the homes of his parishioners from time to time and chant sutras in front of the family *butsudan,* the Buddhist altar, where small mortuary tablets of the deceased are honored. This visitation requires the family members to sit kneeling before the altar as the sutras are droned on, she says with a smile, during which the children often make bored faces or try to silently text their friends.

The rain let up, and I sensed that my time was up as well, so I thanked the priest's wife for the tea, cakes, and conversation and took my leave. As I turned at the temple gate to bow once again, she was still at the top of the steps, bowing to the foreigner who had dropped in wet and unannounced.

As I hiked back up to the Komao, it was clear that all was not well with my feet. It was already four in the afternoon when I arrived back, however, and this was, after all, a hot spring, so I tucked my *yukata* and tiny towel under my arm and headed for the bath. The bathroom itself was cavernous, and the tiled bath itself big enough for at least five or six people. It had been a wet, cold day, and I was the only one here in the bath, so I took my time for a long soak in the hot water. Alas, it was late in the afternoon, so I was unable to follow the advice of the *Ryoko yojinshu*, which suggests the following.

> The method of bathing in a hot spring is the following: For the first day or two, enter the bath three or four times a day. If it feels right, then go anywhere from five to seven times. The old and weak should adjust themselves accordingly.

Nevertheless, I stretched out in the very hot water and, half dozing, remembered two of Santoka's haiku—different moods, but somehow appropriate.

> 一人のさみしさが温泉ひたりて秋の夜
> The loneliness of being by myself,
> soaked in the hot spring:
> an autumn night.

> 朝湯こんこんあふれるまんなかのわたし
> The morning bath bubbling thick and fast;
> and right in the middle?
> Me!

Drying off as well as I could with the thin towel, I stayed in my yukata and *haori*—a mid-sleeve loose coat tied with cords—until dinner, which was served in a spacious dining room on the first floor. There were only five or six guests this evening, and I struck up a conversation with a middle-aged couple who had driven down from Tokyo for the night. He was suffering from a chronic lumbago, he explained, and frequented baths in hot springs to lessen the symptoms. By his smile, I inferred that his "lumbago" was a great excuse to leave Tokyo for hot springs—a few of which he heartily recommended to me—and his wife was a willing accomplice. Soon, our meals were brought out, and we turned our attention to the other pleasure of these resorts, which, here at the Komao, included fifteen different dishes.

At intervals during the meal, the head waiter and I talked about my plans to climb Mount Ontake in a few days, but later the conversation turned to sumo, of which we were both fans. He told me that sumo wrestlers often came to the Komao for R & R, and pointed out a large, wide framed scroll over the entrance to the dining room with red ink handprints of five sumo wrestlers, their signatures below each handprint in black. They had all stayed here some time ago—the famous Chiyonofuji, Takanohana (*père*), and three others—and I now understood the reason for the size of the baths.

Back in my room, I read through the folktales of the Kiso until bedtime—a lot about foxes and their fidelity to benefactors, rather than their usual pranks and habits of bewitching people, and their favorite food: tempura mouse. In all my years in Japan, I have never seen a fox, although I suspect that they have seen me, especially out on the back roads along the rice fields that border the mountains. In Japan, the fox is the messenger of Inari, the god of harvests, and lives in that liminal world between gods and men.

AT SIX IN THE MORNING, the mountains were full of mists, their colors muted to a series of light and dark pastels. The temperature was forecast to be about ten degrees Celsius (fifty Fahrenheit) in the morning and heating up to twenty degrees in the afternoon. The TV weather report was to be followed with a short piece on the newest popular Japanese rock groups, Bump of Chicken and

The Funky Monkey Babies, but I opted to go down for break-fast, which this morning included dessert yogurt, eggs and bacon cooked in a flat pot over a sort of paraffin heater, tangerines, miso soup, rice, and great coffee.

After my third cup of coffee, I went upstairs, packed, took the crumpled newspapers out of my boots, checked the map, and got ready for the road. Thanking the manager and head waiter for their hospitality, I went out the front door to find my friend with the backaches and his wife waiting in their car, and they kindly offered to take me to my next destination, Kiso Fukushima. I politely declined, and we all waved each other good-bye. Later, I would wonder about the wisdom of my decision, but for now I walked back down the hill and in five more minutes was back on the Nakasendo, which shortly joined the national highway again.

This part of the road is perhaps the least scenic on the entire Kiso Road: trucks whizzing by at a high speed, a narrow sidewalk, and defunct roadhouses here and there. Somehow I missed my turnoff where the old road heads out back into a quieter district, but I quickly got a second try and was soon walking through rice fields, past farm houses, and finally over a bridge that crosses the Kiso River—narrower now but still lined with autumnal leaves and rushing over rocks and boulders of every size and shape.

Across this bridge is an old shrine tucked into the mountain and under a dark canopy of maples, cedars, and cryptomeria. Over the sliding entrance door, there is a wooden placard engraved with the characters 荒神, which can generally be interpreted in two ways: pronounced *arakami*, it means a rough and violent god that needs to be appeased by certain festivals and ceremonies; pronounced *kojin*, it is the god of the kitchen. More specifically, my *Kokugo dai-jiten* dictionary defines the god in this way:

> This is a god that protects the Three Jewels of Buddhism: the Bud-dha, the Dharma and the Sangha. He displays anger with three heads and six arms, and is deeply venerated by the members of Shugendo and Nichiren Buddhism. Among the common people

he is respected as the god of the hearth, and by extension, fire. He is also believed to be a god who generally protects agriculture.

Interestingly, the dictionary also notes that his name is used as a synonym for "wife." With that, I returned to the map and found that I could either go just a little farther up the hill and take the old Nakasendo or go down the hill and take the road that follows the river. From where I stood, I could see that the old road was thickly lined with trees and was probably a pleasant walk, but that the one below went along quite close to the river and included some of the loveliest scenery I had seen yet. With a quick but reverent bow to the rough kitchen god, I took the low road and was rewarded with rice fields already harvested and farmhouses bordered by mountains on my right, and the purples, yellows, reds, and browns stretching over and flowing down to the river on my left. This was autumn at its very best. I murmured a thanks to the *arakami/kojin* god and, trying to ignore the pain in my feet, continued on.

Eventually, the road branched off in different directions, and I was lost again. Passing through a neighborhood of houses and up a hill, I stopped to ask an elderly lady tending a garden in her yard for directions. She cheerfully let me know that I was close to my destination and invited me in for tea. I turned her down, with regrets, and in ten minutes the national highway appeared on the hill far above me, leading into a tunnel bypassing the next town. Just above the tunnel was a large sign: "The Kiso Fukushima Barrier." Crossing the river, I turned onto the road that leads into the old post town and passed beneath the huge torii gate that straddles the road. I have always felt at home in this town—the one that Kaibara Ekiken described as "the best town, not only in the Kiso Mountains, but on the entire Shinano Road."

COURSE TIME
Miya no koshi to Kiso Fukushima: 7 kilometers (4.2 miles).
3 hours, 10 minutes.

8 Kiso Fukushima and Mount Ontake

兼山. 曰, 艮, 止成
時止則止, 時行則行.
動静不失其時, 其道光明 . . .
君子以思不出其位.

> *Mountains on top of mountains.*
> *This is* ken *[keeping still], and means to stop.*
> *When it is time to stop, [the Gentleman] stops;*
> *when it is time to go, [the Gentleman] goes.*
> *Thus, motion and peace do not lose their moments.*
> *That is the bright and clear way . . .*
> *Therefore, the Gentleman does not let his thoughts*
> *go beyond his situation.*
>
> —*I-Ching*, hexagram 54

KISO FUKUSHIMA: Elevation 2,370 Feet

Kiso Fukushima was and remains today the largest of the eleven post towns on the Kiso Road, not only because of the imposing barrier here, but also due to its lively commerce. Kaibara Ekiken noted that "all sorts of things are sold here," and Okada Zenkuro reported the following:

> This post town has the most commerce and products for sale in the entire Kiso Valley. The leaders of the community are wealthy. . . . Every year there is a horse market where various kinds of cotton and hemp goods, wooden tools and implements, preserved

mochi, black pepper, dried bracken, rock mushrooms, and salted fish from both the southern and northern seas are sold. It is a prosperous and bustling town. Thus, even people of lower ranks carry on with their livelihoods in a good fashion.

I hobbled past the barrier, situated on the highest point of the northern end of the town, and slowly made my way down the hill into the town proper. The main road, which now joins, now separates from the old Nakasendo threads through a lively area of dry-goods shops, banks, bars, a high-end sake shop, two food markets, and a minipark where travelers can soak their feet in a three-foot-by-six-foot hot spring bordered by cedar planks while the Kiso River rushes by far on the right. Several bridges cross the river to the west side of town, but eventually, as the town thins out, the river broadens and flows rapidly along only a few feet from the road.

A little farther along was my inn, its entrance facing the road, its westernmost rooms right on the river itself. The Sarashina-ya had originally been established in 1872 near the barrier but was torn down and rebuilt at its present location in 1927. It is difficult to tell whether it is a two- or three-story building because of the curious way the stairways wind up and down, but all of the rooms—which are of various sizes—are traditional, with tatami floors and wooden beams. There is at least one scroll of either Japanese scenery or calligraphy on the wall in even the smallest of the rooms, which are generally for two guests. Other rooms will accommodate six to eight people. Mr. Ando, whose ancestors were samurai retainers to the local lord, is the sixth-generation owner of the inn, but his wife, Mineko, actually runs the place with a quiet but very efficient hand. Printed next to her name on her business card is 女将, pronounced *o-kami,* literally meaning "lady general."

Mineko, a tall, handsome woman in her mid-fifties, greeted me at the entranceway with a warm but half-distracted smile. "Gomen nasai, Biru-san," she apologized. "We have a full house—twenty construction workers from Nagoya—so I can't put you in your favorite room over the river. I hope you don't mind." The room she referred to is a large one, enough for four people, overlooking the Kiso River. I once stayed there during a typhoon and watched the waves roil and leap over the boulders midstream, wondering if we weren't all going to take a ride down to the next post town that night. At other times, it has simply been a swiftly flowing current, clear enough to see the bottom and for birds to play along the banks. On the wall of this room hangs a scroll of calligraphy from some Buddhist scripture, and over the door are amulets from Mount Ontake. With the window open at night, sleep comes to the voice of the river, soothing any aches and pains acquired during the day. It is my favorite room on the entire Kiso Road.

But this time I was led up to a small but comfortable room overlooking the road—a road, I reminded myself, people have walked for over a thousand years. Cars, for the most part, have taken the place of straw-sandaled feet, but there are still many of us who take this route on foot.

Soon, Mineko and her daughter appeared at my door with coffee and *mikan,* small Japanese tangerines, and we talked about the plans I had for climbing Mount Ontake. Her husband had arranged for a young artist, Yamashita Katsuhiko, who is also a mountaineer and a practitioner of the Ontake religion, to accompany me, but she had noticed my limp and wondered if I was in any condition for the climb. In her mother-general sort of way, she asked me to take off my socks for a look at my feet, and when I did, we all looked aghast at the sight: large red blisters on top of blisters, both right and left, and for the first time I understood the meaning of the word in Japanese—*mame* (meaning "bean"). Mineko gave me her most serious look, declared the climb to be off, and said that she would call Mr. Yamashita to let him know. I did not struggle with this decision, which had been creeping up on me for a couple of days.

When it is time to stop, the Gentleman stops;
When it is time to go, the Gentleman goes . . .
and does not let his thoughts go beyond his situation.

This done, we chatted for a while longer, coffee was refilled, and Mineko and her daughter—who had recently graduated from college and had come back to help with the inn—made polite apologies for taking up too much of my time ("Nagajiri itashi-mashita"—literally, "We have made long buttocks.") and took their leave. Lunch is generally not served in Japanese inns, so I followed them down, gingerly put my boots back on, and slipped out the entranceway.

It is a short walk along the river back into town and into my favorite coffee shop there, the Jyurin. The proprietress greeted me with a "Welcome back!" and showed me to a seat at a wooden table overlooking the river. This is a small establishment, only five tables with seating for twenty at the most, and is perfectly situated for whiling away an afternoon. The west wall is mostly a sliding glass window, and just beyond the road across the river, the mountain angles up, allowing only a narrow view of the sky. Today, yellow leaves—ginkgo, maybe?—were falling into the clear current and being swept downstream over the blue-gray rocks beneath. A small black-and-white bird, the *sekirei* (a kind of wagtail), flitted quickly and nimbly over the rushing water and exposed boulders. Watching the yellow leaves flow away, I was aware of the maudlin thought of just how many years had gone by, just as fast, disappearing from sight.

The proprietress brought me a bowl of rice topped with shrimp tempura, and a cup of tea, and I quickly had other more immediate things on my mind. Opening my wooden chopsticks and mumbling, "Itadakimasu" ("I humbly receive"), I got to work.

Back at the Sarashina-ya, there was time for a bath. Again, it was early and the other guests were still out, so I could take my time, first washing off, seated on one of the low wooden stools, and then dipping into the one-man wooden tub. It would be easy to fall asleep here, and some people do, although it is not recommended. After thirty minutes, I roused myself, dried off, and got back upstairs for a long nap. Outside, the sky had begun to scud over with clouds, and the temperature had dropped. I turned on my gas heater and drifted away, one more leaf down the stream.

At six thirty, I awoke to Mineko calling me down for dinner. The Sarashina-ya has been a minshuku since it was rebuilt here nearly ninety years ago, so the guests all eat in a large tatami-floored room on the first floor. Cushions are placed around low wooden tables, seating is indicated by room numbers, and the usual numerous dishes are set out ahead of time. Beer and sake are available from a large upright glass cooler at the end of the room. The construction workers filed in and took their places, tired from a day of work. These were tough-looking men but polite and deferential to the lady-general, and I noticed that one of them was wearing a Hello Kitty sweatshirt and sweatpants. "Cute" here in Japan seems to know no social or gender boundaries.

We all eagerly worked through our dishes of fish, vegetables, rice, miso soup, soba, pickles, and tangerines, watched the news on the TV at the other end of the room, and, one by one, returned to our rooms to end the day. I noticed that a number of my inn mates were bringing large bottles of sake up to their rooms with them, but my one bottle of Asahi Draft with dinner would suffice for the night.

Back under the futon, I selected one of the books on local tales from the bookstore in Harano. It includes a short story about a fox at the Kozenji, the most famous temple in Kiso Fukushima.

> In a hamlet just in front of the gate to Kiso Fukushima, there is a temple called the Kozenji. There is a beautiful garden in this temple, and, just inside the garden grounds, there stands a mortuary marker for a fox.
>
> At the beginning of the Meiji period, a fox had shape-shifted into a human being and was serving as a young acolyte at the temple. The abbot was aware that this was really a fox but allowed

him to stay in the temple anyway. Thus, when the little acolyte was taking a nap and carelessly let his tail into view, the abbot would lean down and whisper, "Hey, hey. Your tail is showing."

One day, the abbot sent the little acolyte off with a message to someone in the hamlet of Hiwada. The fox/boy successfully delivered the message to its destination, but on the return road, he was shot with a rifle and killed. When seen with the naked eye, the acolyte had appeared just like a human being, but when sighted down the barrel of a gun, it could be seen that he was nothing but a fox. Because of this, the hunter had taken aim and fired.

The priest waited anxiously for the acolyte and finally became so concerned that he walked to Hiwada himself. On the mountain road, he found the body of the acolyte and carried it back to the temple. There, out of grief, he buried its bones and set up a mortuary marker.

This is said to be the story of the mortuary marker of the fox.

At midnight, I was awakened by Jon Braeley, a friend and independent filmmaker from Miami. He had just come in on the last train from Tokyo with two large suitcases full of camera equipment. I was in such a daze—my head full of foxes, priests, and temple gardens—that I could only welcome him in with a wave from the futon and indicate the closet where his own bedding was stored. I quickly returned back to intermittent sleep until dawn.

BREAKFAST CALL came all too early, and we headed downstairs for a surprise: a Western-style breakfast of eggs, sausage, and toast. Mineko had been thoughtful enough to prepare something more suited, she thought, than the usual fare for her two American guests, and I, for one, enjoyed the change. The Japanese version of toast is always cut about an inch and a half thick and is liberally coated with melting butter. I dug in.

Jon and I talked over the day with several cups of coffee—also there for our exclusive enjoyment. He had just arrived in Japan and had come to film the Japanese National Kendo Tournament but thought it might be interesting to first see some of the area I had recommended to him over the years. His schedule was tight, so we would just have time to look over this little country town before he headed back to Tokyo, one of the largest and most modern cities in the world. Jon is originally from England and is cheerful and talkative—an excellent companion after a number of solo days on the road. The old Japanese saying puts it very simply:

旅は道連れ

For journeys, a companion.

Travel is touted as expanding one's experiences and outlook about the world, but I often fear that in walking alone for too long, my perceptions tend to feed upon themselves and to be satisfied with my own provincial habits and insularity. There is certainly no joy equal to walking through these mountains alone, but I can hardly count the number of times I've had my eyes opened by a casual remark dropped by a fellow traveler. On the other hand, hard experience has shown that you must pick your companions well. In his essay *On Going on a Journey* (1822), William Hazlitt wrote about the unfortunate effects of having the wrong traveling companion during significant moments on one's journey:

> These eventful moments in our lives' history are too precious, too full of solid, heartfelt happiness to be frittered and dribbled away in imperfect sympathy. I would have them all to myself, and drain them to the last drop.

Jon, however, is a filmmaker and, aside from being good-natured and intelligent, has an eye open constantly for what is around him.

The temperature had dropped into the upper forties or lower fifties Fahrenheit, not uncommon for late October in the Kiso Valley, and it was going to be a cold and long walk carrying heavy camera equipment, when we were given another surprise. The preparation and serving of breakfast in the inn being over, Mineko had decided to leave operations to her daughter and suggested (lady-general-like) that we allow her to drive us through town and up the hill to the Fukushima *sekisho*, or barrier. The car was already out in front, she said, so please get in. There was clearly no room for us to argue, even if we had wanted to, and soon, her little car was winding up a very narrow road, bypassing the many stone steps up the 250-foot steep slope atop which the barrier sits. The open wooden building and gates occupy a flat stretch of ground no more than 220 feet long; to the east is the edge of Mount Seki, while to the west, the cliff cascades down to the Kiso River. This was not an easy place to get through unnoticed.

As Jon set up his camera equipment, Mineko, a part-time tour guide, explained that Kiso Fukushima, being just about at the center of the Kiso Valley and midway between Edo and Kyoto, occupied a strategic and essential site in the line of traffic. Thus, it was an extremely appropriate place for establishing a barrier. No one knows when the original barrier was built, but the Nakasendo was "opened" in 1601, so it was probably not long after that. During the period of the Kiso clan domination of the area, smaller barriers had been erected at Niekawa and Tsumago, and likely here, too; but when control of the valley passed into the hands of the Tokugawa, the buildings and gates were strengthened and put under the management of the Yamamura clan, who became the hereditary magistrates.

The length of the barrier runs north-south and hugs the western side of the mountain. Travelers, from warlords and their retinues to commoners, had to wait their turn to go before the official and receive permission to pass through, and at any other season than summer, the delay must have involved much shivering and stamping of feet against the cold. The sun had not yet peeked over the crest of the mountain, and it was more than just a little chilly this mid-autumn morning, so Mineko and I walked inside the unheated edifice, more just to keep moving than from any warmth it might provide.

The structure at this barrier is much like that at Niekawa, only larger and more imposing. We took off our shoes at the open entranceway, a display of various weapons used during Edo times at our left. These include spears, bows, staves, and a curious one with a long wooden handle and two-foot curled barbs at one end. This was for stopping people trying to run through the barrier by snagging their clothes rather than for inflicting any real harm. How people might have thought that they could get by soldiers armed with such weapons waiting at either end of the narrow pathway is not clear.

Inside the otherwise bare room are displays of the wooden passes issued to go through the barrier, documents, old illustrations, and firearms from the period. Originally, this had been an area for guards or servants to rest or simply to wait when they were on call. The next and largest room is open to, and about three feet above, a courtyard of small stones—sand when the barrier was in use—in which is a brazier, a flat cushion, a small desk, and an armrest for the official conducting the inspection of papers and passes. Travelers other than warlords, their retinues, and aristocrats would kneel in the sand awaiting the go-ahead from the official. The room on the farthest end is the small dark room where "boys" would be inspected by an old lady with a large magnifying glass if their sex was in question. There are other very small rooms for things such as delivering tea to the official and his assistants, and a short hallway to the rear of these. Two large wooden gates, north and south, allowed travelers to enter and exit.

On a busy day, the official's tedium would only have been broken by the interesting variety of travelers who were applying to pass through: warlords, *ronin,* farmers on pilgrimages, traveling musicians, poets and actors, businessmen and their assistants, and people of all types just traveling because they could. The Kiso is known for having a culture with elements of both eastern and western Japan, and as the men and women of different classes were forced to wait together in the inns in post towns like Fukushima and Narai, there must have been interesting exchanges of ideas, styles, songs, stories, and even jokes, as travelers and their hosts got a taste of faraway places they would never themselves have passed through. Originally intended to discourage movement, barriers like the one here did more to encourage a flow of ideas and perhaps even a fuller sense of what it was to be Japanese.

Sunlight had started to appear across the river on the crests of Mount Seki, and Jon had finished with a series of photographs of the area, so we began to pack up. As we put Jon's heavy equipment into the tiny trunk of Mineko's car, she explained that this barrier was in operation until February of 1869 and demolished later in an attempt to rid the country of all vestiges of Tokugawa power and influence. The site of the barrier, however, had been excavated in 1975, and its remaining structure and full placement of buildings and design all confirmed by comparing documentary materials. Reconstructed in 1977, it was designated as a national historical site two years later. As we began to leave, Japanese tourists were beginning to climb up the long stone steps (punctuated every ten yards or so by a statue of the bodhisattva Jizo, the protector of travelers) to get a feeling for their own national history—but, no doubt, without the sense of anticipation that their Edo-period ancestors would have felt.

MINEKO'S NEXT STOP was the site of the mansion of the hereditary magistrates of Kiso Fukushima, the barrier, and much of the Kiso Valley in general—the Yamamura clan. The Yamamura were once the vassals of the Kiso clan, but they had fought bravely at

Sekigahara and were consequently ordered to their elevated position by Tokugawa Ieyasu.

We crossed the Otebashi Bridge—the oldest concrete bridge in Japan—and parked in front of the old stone walls that once delineated part of Kiso Castle but now mark what is left of the lower mansion and garden. With the maps extant today, we can imagine the extensive size of the magistrate's palatial mansion during the Edo period—only one-tenth of which remains today. In his travelogue of the Kiso, *Kisoji kiko*, the haiku poet Yokoi Yayu wrote under the year 1745,

> In Fukushima today—the 12th—I was allowed to visit the Yamamura clan's mansion. It was spotlessly clean, and the servants ran around with both upper and lower formal garments, asking what we would like. Spreading out trays of sea bream and yellowtail, it did not feel like a mountain home at all.

俎上のなる日はきがずか鳥
On the day of chopping blocks,
not a trace
of the cuckoo.

The cuckoo is a bird that seeks out solitary places and only sings when it has the leisure to do so.

Mineko, Jon, and I took off our shoes and walked through the preserved remains of the lower mansion, which was reconstructed in 1723 by the thirteenth-generation magistrate. The halls are filled with the costumes, armor, and art of the Edo period, several of the Yamamura having been scholars and artists of some note, and this section of the mansion had had an extensive library as its center. Turning through the hallway, we came upon displays of the meals that were offered to visiting dignitaries, including the fortunate Yokoi Yayu: every seafood imaginable—brought in fresh from both the Pacific and the Sea of Japan—river fish, mountain vegetables, and herbs served on red and black lacquerware trays, plates, and dishes attest to the wealth and prestige of the clan.

According to a map of the mansion dated 1823, there were some twenty-three gardens, and among those, there were five with miniature lakes. To the right, however, through the sliding glass doors, the only remaining garden opens up to the east. Although the leaves on the trees were gone at this time, making it look somewhat forlorn, the garden has a small pond and uses the technique of *shakkei,* or "borrowing scenery," with Mount Komagatake far in the distance. A waterfall falls in cascades into some rapids and then enters the pond, which is surrounded by a number of "guardian rocks." A stone bridge crosses the pond to an island, where a "snow-viewing lantern" has been set. On a small stylized mountain to the left of the waterfall is a Fudo Myo-o stone, which guards the source of the water and watches over it as it passes. This stone also manifests lucky events for the household, which it did well for over two hundred fifty years, and protects the house itself. Behind the waterfall there is a shrine to Inari, and an old lantern is engraved with the date 1782.

The Yamamura seemed to have held Inari, the god of the harvest, in high regard, and one of the last displays to be seen as you walk through the mansion is that of a preserved two-hundred-year-old carcass of a fox—Inari's messenger—enshrined in a small room of its own. As Okada Zenkuro pointed out in a number of places in his report, the Kiso Valley experiences cold temperatures, is surrounded by mountains, and has few level places for agriculture. Thus, the harvest god and her messengers were held in great esteem, and, no doubt, fried tofu—one of the foxes' favorite dishes—was often set out in places where the furry animals were known to pass by.

Before we piled back into Mineko's car, she pointed out the stone on the old fortifications on which the above haiku by Yayu (page 105) was engraved. As I posed with Mineko for the de rigueur commemorative photograph, I couldn't help thinking of the poet's lucky day at this once-huge mansion. Yayu was a man of the samurai class, had founded a school of military science, and was a senior bureaucrat in charge of the castles at Edo, Osaka, and Kyoto. But the cultured Yamamura were likely most pleased to have him there in his capacity as a famous writer of haiku and later recited his commemorative poem with satisfaction and pride.

Another poem, with an introduction, by Yayu shows his more sensitive side and may indicate the direction of the conversation that day:

> At the hottest time of the year, it was difficult to bear, and I hummed verses to myself about the cicadas and the heat. But the days passed by, and soon their voices grew weaker in the autumn wind, and I began to feel sorry for them.

> 死にのこれ一つばかりは秋の蟬
> May at least one of them
> remain alive:
> autumn cicadas.

> We cannot say that people are really living if they are not also living within nature, that is, living within the garden. Gardens play an important role in our health, just as in olden times there was the saying, "In houses where gardeners come and go, there is no need for the doctor." The garden is essential to our life, and not something we can do without.
>
> —Mirei Shigemori, *Modernizing the Japanese Garden*

Our last stop for the morning was the Kozenji, one of the five temples in Kiso Fukushima and one of the three most famous in the Kiso Valley. Well known as the family temple for both the Kiso and Yamamura clans, it was built in 1434 by Kiso Nobumichi for the Buddhist memorial services for his ancestors, although the temple itself must predate this by centuries. Now under the Zen Buddhist order, it was likely first established as a Tendai or Shingon temple in the eleventh century, for in front of the main hall is a weeping cherry tree said to have been planted as a seedling by Yoshinaka himself. Mineko, Jon, and I slowly walked up the graded approach to the temple, passing by a huge flat rock, supposedly for practicing Zen meditation. On our left was a large statue of Jizo comforting two children and, farther up the walkway, six smaller statues of Jizo, one for each of the six realms through which we transmigrate.

Mr. Ando's ancestors are also memorialized here, so Mineko passed through the gate separating the walkway from the temple, spoke quickly with the attendant priest, and on her return, informed us that there would be no entry fee.

On our way through the gate, a young priest with shaven head and informal beige baggy pants and upper garment stood in the entrance to the main temple on our right. He greeted us with a silent nod and withdrew into the dark interior.

Facing the main entrance to the temple is the expansive "dry garden" created by the garden master Shigemori Mirei in 1963, called the Kan'untei 看雲庭, "Garden for Observing the Clouds." Extending out from the front of the main hall, the garden contains a large flat area of small pebbles, broken up by three groups of fifteen rocks of various sizes. The pebbles are raked in broad curving patterns out into the four directions, suggesting a sea of clouds, while the dark rocks appear to be the peaks of mountains rising above those clouds. These "peaks" are arranged in asymmetrical groups of seven, five, and three—*shichigosan* in Japanese—the three ages considered critical for children and the ages when they are taken to a shrine on November 15 to ask for the gods' protection. The entire effect is one of movement and change within empty, still space. The garden itself is enclosed by a white wall topped with dark tiles and, beyond that, a few large trees now with red and orange leaves. Even farther beyond are the mountains rising from the other side of the post town. Concerning his gardens, Mirei wrote,

> If what the gods made is nature, then the garden is the part that the gods forgot to make. So it is up to us to take the place of the gods and make gardens. We ourselves must become gods.

Mirei was a native of Okayama Prefecture who studied tea ceremony and flower arranging in his teens. In college he studied Japanese painting, art history, and philosophy, courses and interests that would eventually lead him to a life of creating gardens. Almost all of his gardens—which grace shrines, temples, castles, and even a town hall—are in the style of *karesansui,* or "dry landscape," Zen influenced but at the same time quite modern. On this cloudless day, the contrasts between the apparent movement of the white pebbles and the primordial stability of the dark rocks are astonishing. Confucius wrote,

本立而道生
When the foundation is established, intelligent movement is born.

Mountains and the flowing clouds: stability and movement. I tried to imagine how Mirei first conceived of this remarkable creation but brushed the thought aside. That is not the point here. The very name of the Kan'untei is instructive of how it should be viewed, after all: the first character 看, *kan,* depicting a hand held over the eyes, like a person looking into the broad distance, not into a scramble of thoughts.

Jon and Mineko had finished up trying to take photographs of the garden. "I have lived here for so many years," she exclaimed with mild exasperation, "but still can't get it right." Jon just screwed up his face with a funny smile as if to ask, "How *do* you get something like this?"

Before we left, we found the entrance to the much smaller Edo-period garden to the south and rear of the main temple.

Compared to the Kan'untei, this garden is cramped and crowded with moss, bushes, trees, and even a tiny stream or pond—hard to tell which—with a stone slab bridge. The vegetation is meticulously cared for here—each bush and tree kept at a certain shape and size—and while the garden is clearly a harmonious whole, attention can be paid to each element that creates that whole. The eye moves from tree to bush, some red with autumn, others evergreen, but with composure rather than in haste. After a short quiet moment, we moved on.

IT HAD BEEN a long morning, and Mineko was expected back at the inn to begin preparations for the evening meal. With apologies, she dropped Jon and me off in the old part of the post town, an interesting area with winding narrow streets and wooden houses of traditional architecture. We passed by a fountain made of two wooden pipes emptying water into a wooden basin, which a faded sign declared it had been doing continuously for the last five hundred years. Around the corner was the site of the old signboard that advised travelers of what they needed to know about the town. The street—this was the old Kiso Road again—wound down the hill through lacquerware shops that have been in business since the Edo period and then past the city hall, the site of the old honjin. In the rear garden behind the city hall stands a stone slab engraved with a haiku from Basho.

さざれ蟹足這のぼる清水かな
Skinny crab
legs crawling
out of the pure water.

This monument once stood upright in the middle of a vegetable field where clear water bubbled up from the ground, but it was moved to its present site in 1953. When or why it was originally placed in the vegetable field is unknown.

In this part of town, or near it, is the site of the old castle built by Kiso Yoshiari. It was a typical Warring States–period fortification with a moat, winding streets, and a reservoir but was burned to the ground, and the site is now occupied by Kiso Fukushima Elementary School. Looking up this locale lost out to hunger, however, so the two of us made our way back to the coffee shop for lunch, watched the leaves carried by the river go by, and then headed home. Jon had editing work to do, and I was ready for another long, hot bath and a nap. On the way to the inn, I could not pass up buying some tasty Japanese tangerines, then in season, at a local grocery store. *Mikan* are sweet, the peel is loose and easy to remove, and we managed to finish the entire bag off soon after settling in to our room.

With early evening, we were called down to dinner with the construction workers, and Jon generously ordered a large bottle of sake, which went well with the grilled river fish, the thick, sweet miso sauce on steamed eggplant, rice, a variety of vegetables, and miso soup. Back up in our room, he ordered yet another bottle, and we finished off the evening exchanging stories of living and traveling in Japan, Miami, and elsewhere in the world. I was greatly entertained with his accounts of the recent Halloween being enthusiastically celebrated in bars and nightclubs in Tokyo and how young ladies there dressed as Raggedy Ann, Cinderella, and French waitresses, while the men wore costumes of pirates and Pokemon. We had started the day with the ancient traditional barrier and ended it up with tales of the modern and open urban life. Japan, it seems, cannot and will not be held in a single state of mind.

THE MORNING WAS BRIGHT AND CLEAR, with only a slight chill in the air. Jon and I ate a full breakfast with the workers from

Nagoya—the one was still dressed in his Hello Kitty sweatpants and shirt—and then walked up the hill to the train station. Jon was heading back to Tokyo to film the National Kendo Tournament, and I was taking the day off from hiking and going the opposite direction, to the town of Nakatsugawa to cash some traveler's checks. I arrived at my destination in an hour, and waiting for me was my old friend Ichikawa-san, nearly eighty now with long, thin hair, a sparse beard, and an almost-disarming twinkle in his eye. He has looked more and more like a *sennin,* or "mountain sage," every time we've met—the effect, no doubt, of a lifetime spent hiking the mountains and reading classical Oriental literature.

After catching up, Ichikawa-san drove me to the bank, and I changed my traveler's checks into Japanese yen, an increasingly difficult transaction. Although I was now ready for some good conversation at a coffee shop, when I stepped back into the car, my friend, ever the observant mountaineer, noticed that I was walking with a pronounced limp. So, instead of the comfort of a coffee shop, he drove me to a local clinic to check out the blisters and so ward off any future disasters.

> When people who are not used to travel become tired or get blisters on their feet, it is entirely because they have put on their footwear indifferently. Get good footwear, have them properly worn in, and do not hurriedly put them on. Make sure that they are neither too tight nor too loose. Again, when your feet are desiccated, hot, and thus cause you discomfort, you will get blisters. At such times, loosen the ties of your footwear now and again, cool your feet, and rest in a proper posture.
>
> —*Ryoko yojinshu*

Soon I was seated in a small office while a young Dr. Saito examined my feet. He was clearly impressed—as were the nurses—with the size and number of blisters but pronounced me to be OK and advised a full day of rest. Taking a good look at the callous on my left big toe, however, he expressed a bit of curiosity as to how it got there and asked how long I'd had it. I explained that I practiced kendo—Japanese fencing—back in Miami, and he nodded approval and laughed. The nurses looked quizzical, so he stood up from his chair, grabbed an imaginary bamboo sword, and, in white coat and stethoscope, lunged around the small room two or three times, pushing off appropriately with his left foot. "Daigaku no jidai, sandan deshita yo." ("In college, I was a third-degree blackbelt.") We all laughed, and I limped out into the waiting room, to find Ichikawa-san wondering what all the stamping was about. "Excellent technique," I explained, and off we went to a local Indian restaurant—dal with spinach, chicken curry, and mango juice—accented with an hour's worth of reminiscences about our climbs together. Then it was back to the station, a heart-felt good-bye, and the return trip to Kiso Fukushima. In less than two hours, I was back at the Sarashina-ya, where I washed and dried more clothes and took a nice soaking bath. Later that evening I had a quiet dinner—Jon and the Nagoya workmen were all gone—and was off to bed.

MOUNT ONTAKE: Elevation 10,067 Feet

Not far from Kiso Fukushima stands the 10,067-foot Mount Ontake, one of the holiest mountains in Japan. Although it is only distantly visible from a few points along the Kiso Road, it dominates the spiritual landscape and is in some way there in the consciousness of everyone living in the post towns along this ancient route. During the summer months, the trails leading to the various summits are dotted with white-clad pilgrims, praying as they climb—walking as a religious rite. Although a very few may make the journey to the foothills on foot from their homes elsewhere in Japan, most will take cars or buses to one of the stations from which the trails to the top begin. Such buses or hired cars can be boarded at the train station at Kiso Fukushima, the trip taking forty-five minutes to an hour.

In early October of 1979, I was invited by my friend Ichikawa-san, a seasoned mountaineer, to make a day climb of Mount Ontake and readily agreed. I was staying at the Sarashina-ya, and he picked me up soon after breakfast in his small but comfortable Suzuki sedan. It was a clear day, cool for September, and as we drove along the foothills, we chatted about the origins of Ontake-kyo, or the Ontake religion.

According to Ichikawa-san, Ontake-kyo is not so much a centrally organized religion but is divided into a number of spiritual fraternities, or *kou* 講, each headed by a set of leaders and subleaders and often accompanied by a shaman. My friend further explained that, in this religion, belief is not as important as practice, and that practice centers around prayers to the gods of the mountains, recitation of various sutras, and climbing the mountain itself. At certain times, a group makes an ascent, and individuals will ask an accompanying shaman, who will become possessed by one of the gods and guided by a priest, questions of deep importance to them. These are deeply religious experiences, and the shaman is often physically and psychologically exhausted by such possession. On the way to the Kaida Plateau, where we parked the car and started our walk, we passed a number of small, clean graveyards containing the spirits of believers from the past.

At the Kaida Plateau, the trailhead for the climb, there is a large concrete building complete with comfortable benches, tables, chairs, snacks, and coffee, and a stunning view of the four peaks of the mountain, which has been worshipped since at least the seventh century. Only monks were permitted to climb it until the eighteenth century, when it was "opened" by the ascetic Kakumei, who likely would have blanched at the convenience with which we approached the mountain today.

Kakumei's feelings aside, Ichikawa-san and I left the car in the parking lot, climbed the steps up to the rest station, and indulged in one more cup of coffee to get us on our way. A sign next to the exit encouraged us to use the facilities so as to have no chance to pollute the sacred mountain. This is not just for the hikers' comfort; the practitioners of Ontake-kyo believe that the natural phenomena they personally experience on the mountain—the rocks, grasses, trees, and even the clouds and wind—are the abode and work of the gods and buddhas. This is a deeply felt and sincere belief, and not one to be taken lightly.

Our ablutions complete, we headed out, our only gear being light packs containing water bottles and snacks of rice crackers. The trail from the Kaida Plateau begins as a rocky, mildly sloping incline but quickly becomes steeper and steeper; small stunted trees surround the path, their roots sometimes providing footholds or a kind of riprap. Not far along, there is a small wooden structure, where a priest sells various amulets, talismans, and scrolls depicting the gods of the mountain, one of which I purchased and tucked securely into my pack. Continuing to climb, we sometimes passed groups of various sizes, pilgrims clad in white—including young children and the elderly—all helping each other along. "Gambatte ne!" ("Keep at it!") Farther up the trail, we came across five or six pilgrims making mudras—symbolic symbols with their fingers—chanting mantras, and clapping to get the gods' attention at one of the many sacred shrines along the way. Over the centuries, Ontake-kyo developed from a mixture of ancient mountain worship, Shinto, and esoteric Buddhism, and the influences of all of these are apparent at these sites. Here, there is a shrine dedicated to a Shinto deity; farther up, one enclosing a Buddhist saint; yet beyond that will be a statue of En no Gyoja, the founder of the Shugendo sect. Perhaps most prominent, though not necessarily in size, are the sites holy to Fudo Myo-o, the "Brightness King of Unwavering Mind," an avatar of the Mahavairochana, the "Great Sun Buddha." Holding a sword in his right hand to cut through our ignorance, he also carries a rope in his left to tie up our passions. As Ontake-kyo is a religion that syncretizes Shinto and Buddhism, Fudo Myo-o is also mystically related to Amaterasu Omikami, the sun goddess from whom the Japanese emperors descend. Thus, almost every step on this mountain participates in a mysterious liminal realm.

Gambatte ne! Keep at it!

The two of us continued on, sometimes passing up other climbers and pilgrims, once or twice passed up ourselves by groups of three or four octogenarian ladies all dressed in white, grasping their walking sticks, tiny rucksacks slung over their backs. They smiled and encouraged us to carry on and then disappeared around the next curve.

Stopping at each shrine where there were no pilgrims praying, we clapped our hands reverently to the gods in gratitude and respect. The dwarf conifers and pines had given out some time ago, so we trudged on over the rocky surface under a clear blue sky. After about four and a half hours, we finally reached the caldera of the old volcano. I had been smelling something sour for a while and, looking down into the crater, now understood why: plumes of fine sulfuric steam were rising from three or four places down inside, creating a vision of an entrance to hell. I nervously asked Ichikawa-san if this "dormant" volcano was maybe just a little bit more than that, but he laughed and informed me that there had never been an eruption in recorded history and that geologic evidence suggested that the last volcanic activity had been over six thousand years ago. I did not find the number "six thousand" to be very reassuring in terms of geologic time and suggested that I was ready to go back down. But no, first we hiked over to the main shrine on the peak, prayed to the gods of the mountain (you can imagine what my prayer was about), and then all too slowly headed back down.

On the drive back to the inn, Ichikawa-san told me about the flora and fauna of the Ontake area, some of the former of which are collected and made into small pills called *hyakusogan,* taken for everything from headaches to hangovers to stomach problems. They are supposed to be quite effective, and we stopped at a local store and bought a bottle each. As to the fauna, the most interesting perhaps are the koi that live in a small pond located near the base of Mount Ontake. Thanks to the spiritual quality of the surroundings, they live unbelievably long lifespans. One of these carp, named Hanako, died here in 1977 at the great age of 227, making her the oldest known vertebrate animal in recorded history. I asked Ichikawa-san about maybe stopping to take a sip from the pond, but, alas, it was not on our route.

Back at the Sarashina-ya, we shared a bottle of sake and a fine dinner prepared by Mineko and talked about the day. Ichikawa-san then drove back home, and I took a good long bath and crawled under my futon.

Two weeks later, I was home in Miami, drinking a cup of coffee at my cluttered desk. Picking up the newspaper, I found an article that caught my attention. On October 28, the supposedly dormant volcano Mount Ontake erupted, sending huge clouds of black smoke into the sky, and was expected to continue volcanic activity for some time. I looked up at the scroll of Fudo Myo-o and the gods of Mount Ontake hanging on my wall, said a brief prayer of thanks, and decided that my break time was over.

A NUMBER OF YEARS LATER, I was back in the Kiso and once again staying at the Sarashina-ya. There was a knock on the door of my room announcing dinner, but rather than Mineko, it was her husband, Ando-san. (Mineko has explicitly requested that I call her by her given name; Ando-san is a bit more reticent and shy and prefers his family name.) Dinner was ready, he said, but added that sometime later there would be a service at the local Ontake-kyo temple and asked if I would like to attend. He himself, although a shaman, would be unable to enter the temple as his second granddaughter had just been born, making his presence taboo. I assured him that I would be more than pleased and followed him down to the dining hall.

The dining room was crowded that night, so for convenience's sake, Mineko had put me at the same table as the only other foreigner there, a fiftyish man from the States. As we talked over dinner, he informed me that he was a travel writer and was preparing an article on the Kiso area. Although he spoke almost no Japanese and seemed to be picking at the local food, he was gamely following parts of the Nakasendo, so I quickly let him know about the service at the temple and encouraged him to come along. He was not particularly enthusiastic, but I persisted, and, after our repast, we found ourselves in Ando-san's car, heading toward the temple on the outskirts of the post town. Soon, we were dropped off at the entrance to the temple, our gracious driver telling us that he would pick us up at the conclusion of the service.

The Hyakumataki temple is a wood and clay structure with a gray tiled roof, and not very large—certainly not as large as some of the more elegant Zen and Shin temples that dot the Nakasendo. Inside, cushions were set on the floor for perhaps forty to fifty people at the most and, facing these, a platform on which, this evening, along with two huge dark wooden statues of the men who "opened" the mountain, was a very large polygonal stack of cedar planks, each about a foot and a half long and an inch and a half square. Above this stack of planks hung the holy white folded papers indicating the sacred in the Shinto religion.

As we all entered the temple, we were each given a white jacket to symbolize purity of mind and a cedar plank of our own. This would be an *o-harai,* a ceremony of cleansing. My American acquaintance and I were ushered to the front row of cushions, on each of which was a booklet of sutras written in Sino-Japanese that would be chanted throughout the ceremony. Soon, when the last of the congregation had been seated, a white-robed priest and his attendants mounted the platform, and the chanting began. At first only the priest chanted, his attendants blowing conch shells and beating small drums, but later we were all to join in, and the chanting became faster and more intense. Suddenly, the cedar planks were ignited into a huge bonfire, the priest seemed to go into a trance, and the accompaniment grew louder and louder. I was doing my best to keep chanting along with the unfamiliar sutras, but they were being recited faster and faster, until finally we got to the Hannya shin-gyo, or Heart Sutra, with which I was familiar. Glancing over at my companion, I could see that he was staring straight ahead and looking more than a little uncomfortable.

Throughout the ceremony, the participants had been rubbing the cedar sticks they had received on the part of their bodies that had been causing them trouble—on their heads, for example, if they had had headaches or worries, on their abdomens in the case of stomach pains, or near their eyes if having sight problems. In my case, I had been rubbing my left leg with my stick as we chanted along, hoping to ease the limp I had developed on this hike.

Now, one by one, as the chanting grew more intense, each member individually mounted the platform, bowed to the fire, threw his or her stick into the leaping flames, and the priest then whispered to him some spiritual advice. My turn came. I crawled up in front of the fire, made my obeisance, tossed in my stick, and leaned toward the priest, as he whispered in my ear, "Kaze wo hikanai yo ni, ne. Kiso wa goku samui yo." "Don't catch a cold, now. The Kiso's really cold!" This was not exactly what I expected, but it was certainly thoughtful of him, and I bowed and crawled back down to my cushion. Next it was my companion's turn, but when I motioned to him to go up, he shook his head no. I encouraged him again but got the same stiff response and so explained to the usher that he would not be participating. The usher gave me a quizzical look but then moved on to the next member of the congregation, and I joined back in with the Heart Sutra—thankful that this was the one repeated over and over during the o-harai.

Finally, the flames died down, the priest gave a short homily, and the temple was empty again. Outside, Ando-san was waiting for us and drove us back to the inn as we chatted about our experience. On the way up to our rooms, I asked my American companion, who was still looking a bit stiff and silent, why he hadn't joined in. This had been, after all, a great opportunity to get at travel writing from the inside. "No," he said, "I'm an Episcopalian," and shut his door.

Back in my own room, I couldn't sleep. I felt oddly cleansed and, even though it was going on toward midnight, filled with energy. Sitting on my miniscule couch for a while, I thought over the evening's events and wondered what difference it makes what a person worships, as long as it's curative and for the good. Outside my window, the Kiso River rushed by in swirls and eddies, on its long way to the sea.

Now that my blisters had gone down a bit, I was regretting that I would not be making the climb up Mount Ontake this year but was thankful for the rest. Kiso Fukushima is the halfway point of the Kiso Road, and although I hadn't been breaking any speed records, I was happy to have had a day of catching my breath.

After the television weather report—predicting the day to be clear and unseasonably warm—there was a program on expert coffee making and competition, which I watched with intense interest, remembering my humbling lesson on tea making when I first arrived in Japan. My apartment had been in a small local neighborhood of Buddhist image carvers, a public bath, and a tiny tea store run by a middle-aged man who was missing a front tooth and with a perpetual three-day beard long before it became fashionable. Entering his shop, I had asked for some of his very best tea and been greeted by a blank stare and the question, "Do you know how to make it?" Slightly taken aback, I had replied, "Of course. You boil water and pour it over the tea." He then asked me to wait a minute or two, patiently boiled water in a cast iron tea kettle, let the water cool until he could touch the bottom of the kettle with the palm of his hand, filled a small tea pot with *gyokuro*—the highest grade tea—and poured what seemed to be only two or three sips into a small porcelain teacup. "Don't gulp," he said, knowing that that was exactly what I was going to do. Slowly emptying the cup, I could taste nothing until a subtle aftertaste seemed to go right up the back of my head. I was dumbfounded. Apologizing for my presumptuousness and thanking him for taking the time to provide me with such an exquisite experience, I ordered a small paper bag of an appropriate tea for everyday drinking. As I bowed my way out of the door, he gave me a polite smile and continued his work. This had been the first but not the last lesson I would learn about the extreme care and thoughtfulness the Japanese take in what might seem to be the most commonplace affairs—making tea and coffee included.

After jettisoning some more superfluous clothes and repacking my backpack, I headed down to the foyer, where I met Ginny Tapley Takemori and her husband, Tadashi. Ginny had been one of my editors at Kodansha International and is now a translator and writer; Tadashi is a physicist teaching at a university north of Tokyo. Both are avid hikers. When Ginny had heard that I was coming to Japan for the walk, she volunteered to accompany me for a two-day portion, and I was pleased to have their cheerful company, but at the same time worried that I might slow them down. I explained about the status of my feet, but they were undeterred, and, after tea and cookies provided by Mineko, we thanked our hosts and walked out onto the Kiso Road.

The road out of Kiso Fukushima soon connected with the national highway, but the river was rushing along noisily down to our right, the mountains coming right down to the river were full of color, and the air was still cool and clear. As elsewhere, the Kiso Road now paralleled, now diverged from the national high-way, and the three of us even found some smaller paths that had been a part of the original road in the distant past. After an hour of hiking, we came upon a juncture where the highway was being renovated—this was marked by a hundred or so football-sized yel-low rubber ducks attached to the side rail—and we turned off to a smaller road marked by a wooden sign announcing it as the "Old Nakasendo." There we discovered a narrow footpath through some vegetable gardens leading up to a tiny shrine enclosing a barely visible statue of Batto Kannon dedicated to Kiso Yoshinaka's horse. This horse had been able to understand human speech, it is said, and had been remarkably powerful as well. But when Yoshinaka had given it the command to jump up to a cliff, he—Yoshinaka—had mistaken the distance. The horse jumped exactly as far as Yoshinaka had commanded but missed the cliff due to Yoshinaka's mistake and had fallen to its death. Yoshinaka grieved for the horse and set up the Batto Kannon shrine to pray for its salvation. According to a signboard next to this diminutive edifice, the original shrine had been established a mile or so from its present location but then moved intact with the construction of the Chuo-sen.

After another half hour along the national highway, we arrived at another "Pray to Mount Ontake from Afar" location, but by this time clouds had gathered, and the sacred mountain could not be seen. Still, there were a few pilgrims who had stopped their cars and were praying, their joined hands clasping their rosaries, and their gazes off into the distance. Observing the dedication and faith of these people, I once again regretted not having been able to make the climb.

Finally, as the cliffs along the river became higher and higher, we arrived at the site of the Kiso Road's most famous *kakehashi,* or "suspension bridge," a "bridge" that did not span the river but ran along sideways, parallel to the precipice. From the year 1400 to 1410, a new road had been opened along the Kiso River, and it is said that three hundred fifty feet of wooden planks held together with vines and ropes had been suspended along the cliff. This kakehashi had been repaired repeatedly over the years, but in 1599, Toyotomi Hideyori commanded one of his generals to do major repair. This would be the bridge that had so frightened travelers that their knees shook as they crossed from one end to the other.

Then, in April of 1647, a wayfarer accidentally dropped a pine torch while crossing the bridge, and it burned up completely and collapsed. Consequently, the Yamamura and Chimura clans were given orders and monies from the Owari fief to build a stone wall along the cliff for the bridge, and this was completed the following year. Even today, there remains an engraving, visible in the cliff wall, that states, "This rock wall completed in the sixth month of 1648." Rock wall or not, it must have continued to terrify those who walked across it. The poet Basho crossed the bridge in 1688 at the age of fifty-four and wrote,

> 桟やいのちをからむ蔦かづら
> The suspension bridge!
> One's life entangled
> in vines and creepers.

His disciple Etsujin added,

> 桟ヤ先ずおもひいず馬むかへ
> The suspension bridge!
> The first thing you think of:
> meeting a horse halfway.

In 1741 there was yet another extensive repair and innovation. Then, in 1879, a certain Iseya Denbei built a bridge to the opposite shore, on which pilgrims to Mount Ontake from Owari and Mino paid a fee and were allowed to cross over. The bridge had been fashioned after the Great Bridge at Sanjo in Kyoto and had a balustrade in the elaborate Chinese T'ang dynasty style. The bridge itself was some 190 feet long and 11 feet wide. Unfortunately, it was washed away in a flood on the sixteenth day of the seventh month in 1884, and passengers were reduced to making the difficult passage across the river by boat once again.

Again, however, in 1910, another bridge was built by a private citizen on the same spot as the one that had washed away, using the newest construction techniques of wire ropes. The fare was set at two *sen*. Nonetheless, forty years later the bridge was deemed to be unsafe, and the authorities built a new bridge of the same design on the same spot. Finally, the current bridge was constructed in 1963, and it is this bridge that Ginny, Tadashi, and I crossed to the other side of the Kiso.

The area here is full of ancient trees—chestnuts and pine—and unopened chestnuts litter the path. Dominating the immediate view is a huge stone marker donated by Admiral Togo, noting that the emperor Meiji stopped to rest here. There are also two memorial stones engraved with haiku by Basho and Shiki. It is surprising to know that Shiki, whose health was always so delicate, could put up with the rigors of the Kiso Road, but in 1881, at the age of twenty-five, he traveled the road and wrote the following entry in his *Kakehashi no ki*.

Just at that time there was an early summer shower on my Kiso journey. As I stepped out of my inn, the rain temporarily let up. Taking this moment and hurrying along, I was still chased by passing showers; then, taking a break under the trees, the rain would stop again. At any rate, I went along, being made sport of by the rain, until I reached the suspension bridge. At the sight of them, both cliffs looked quite dangerous, appearing to have been axed out perhaps forty or fifty feet high like a folding screen. The moss seemed to have been growing there in the moist air since the age of the gods, its light green covering spotted casually here and there with azaleas—a scene that could have been painted by artists from the Kano or Tosa schools. Taking a step forward and looking down, the force of the river swollen by the early summer rains swirled in waves struck by currents of cloudy mists, the echoes of which reverberated against the huge crags so that when I returned to the teahouse, sat down on a folding stool, and closed my eyes, the ground continued to shake for a little while.

I went to pay my respects to old Basho's stone monument and crossed the tiny rainbowlike bridge as though I myself were floating in the ether. The soles of my feet felt cold, and I was unable to step along with a good stride; but looking about, I was able to see the traces of the old suspension bridge. I had known about the place before, but today, with the rocks piled up one on top of another, coming and going was carefree from the very start. Still, the ancient scenery must have been one of twisting and crawling vines and creepers.

かけはしやあぶない処に山つづじ
The suspension bridge!
At this dangerous spot,
mountain azaleas.

かけはしや水へとどかず五月雨
The suspension bridge!
The river is never filled:
early summer rains.

むかしたれ雲のゆききのあとつけて
わたしそめけん木曽のかけはし
Long ago,
who would follow along
the coming and going of clouds?
But I'll give it a try
on the Kiso no kakehashi.

About one and a half kilometers from the site of the old bridge, there is a confluence of the Kiso River and the Shinchaya River. During the Meiji period, there had been a teahouse here—the Yayoi Teahouse—where travelers would stop to drink tea and sample the local delicacy, bracken mochi. The following story is still told.

A long time ago, on the bank of the Shinchaya River, there was a teahouse called the Yayoi Teahouse, and one day a mendicant priest stopped to drink tea while resting from his travels. Just then, a man passing by stopped to talk with the master of the teahouse.

"Hey, did you see it? A pumice stone floating down the river again?"

"Sure, I saw it," the master replied. "We'll be lucky if something bad doesn't happen again."

The priest heard these remarks and promptly asked, "What's this business about a pumice stone and the something bad happening?"

According to what the teahouse master said, there was a stone that floated along the river from the suspension bridge to Nezame no Toko, and just as you started thinking how strange that was, the stone would immediately return to the suspension bridge. The master then explained in detail how when this stone made its appearance in the river, someone would inevitably drown, or there would be some other unfortunate occurrence.

The priest then said, "I've done ascetic practices from journey to journey for a long time, but this is the first time I've ever heard of anything like this. I'll try to do something to stop this stone with the strength I've gained from my training."

So saying, he took a brush from the ink-and-brush case at his waist and wrote down a poem on a narrow strip of thick paper.

> The thread connecting
> the bridge and teahouse
> stop the flow
> of the floating
> stone.

The words "bridge" and "teahouse" were written in secret words to help the spell.

Just as the priest had said, as soon as the words were written down, an invisible thread stretched out, the strange floating pumice stone no longer floated down the river, and unlucky events no longer occurred in the village.

It is said that the stone remains today in the upper reaches of the *oni no fuchi*, "Demon's Abyss."

The three of us followed along a narrow road overlooking the river, crossed a bridge parallel to one once used as an old narrow-gauge railroad, and walked into Agematsu. There is a nice little restaurant across from the railroad station, and we stepped inside for sushi and beer to pick up our spirits. The master of the place was a little surprised to find that two of his three guests were foreigners with backpacks who spoke Japanese—Agematsu is not exactly a cosmopolitan town—but welcomed us with a smile and seemed to have understood our predisposition for cold beer even before we had walked in. In seconds, we were *kanpai*-ing to a good day's walk. We made short work of our sushi and headed on to the Sakaju Inn and the ever-smiling o-kami-san, the seventy-nine-year-old Mrs. Hotta.

COURSE TIME
10 kilometers (6.25 miles). 3 hours.

The Lower Kiso

*The current of the moving river is unending, but the water is
never the same. The bubbles floating in the eddies now vanish,
now appear, but there is no example of them lasting for long.
The men of this world and their lodgings are also like this. . . .
Thus, men and their lodgings fight against impermanence,
and if I were to give an example, it would be the dew on the
morning glory. Perhaps the dew falls and the flower remains;
but though we say it remains, it dries in the morning sun. Or
perhaps the flower wilts and the dew does not vanish; but though
we say it does not vanish, it does not wait the coming night.*

—Hojoki

AGEMATSU is and has been a prosperous post town since
ancient times—Kaibara Ekiken found the scenery to be "excep-
tionally beautiful"—when it was managed by the Owari clan.
Traditionally, it has been a lumber collection and distribution
center for Kiso's "five trees"—Japanese cypress, Japanese arborvitae, Hiba arborvitae, Sawara cypress, and Kouyama cedar. Currently, half of the Kiso's Japanese cypress is collected here, and the
town is filled with the aroma of the trees, as are others in the near
area. Formerly, logs were floated down the Kiso River to Nagoya
as rafts, but these days they are transported by trucks and train.
Stacked in large piles—huge trees of reddish-brown bark—they
dominate one's visual and olfactory senses. Perhaps because of the
heavy presence of lumber, Agematsu has suffered fires a number of

times, including the Great Fire of 1950, in which most of the town was burned to the ground. Thus, new buildings are the standard, the atmosphere of the old post town remains in only a few unexpected spots, and there is almost no way of knowing what a bustling town this once was, with over thirty inns. An old children's song that is still sung has it this way:

> When you've gone past Fukushima,
>   you've gone past the temples;
> When you've gone past Agematsu,
>   you've gone past the storehouses;
> When you've gone past Suhara,
>   you've gone past the day laborers.

At the Sakaju, Ginny, Tadashi, and I settled into our rooms of traditional Japanese design and took a brief rest. The inn has been operated by the Hotta family since the Meiji Restoration and was once the stay-over place of Ernest Satow, the famous British diplomat, linguist, and mountaineer in the late 1890s. At that time it had been in a slightly different location and was moved to where it currently stands with the construction of the highway.

We did not rest for long. No more than five minutes after our arrival, Mrs. Hotta offered to walk us to the Gyokurinji, a Rinzai Zen temple established in Agematsu in 1579. Although we were tired from the day's walk, we quickly got up and soon found ourselves walking along a narrow back road, part of the old Kiso Road. Only the beautiful old main gate remains of the original temple, which had been consumed by the fire in 1950, and the rest of the compound is new and quite grand. Across from the main hall is the Thousand Kannon-do, a small shrine with 670 statues of Kannon dedicated so far. The statues are gold-plated, about one and a half feet tall, and placed on three walls of the shrine. Though there are no electric lights inside, the overall effect is one of brilliance. The room is meant to give the impression that Kannon is radiating her compassion to all the billions of worlds in the universe and that this is the only light we may need.

After a while, we were ushered into the back room of the main temple, where all of the mortuary tablets are kept—hundreds of them, each for a local family and their ancestors. It is a part of the chief priests' roles to pray for the souls of the dead, and their descendants will visit the temple on certain days for special prayers (and donations). The current chief priest, who is the eighteenth generation here and distantly related to Mrs. Hotta, is a young man, perhaps in his early forties, and he kindly showed us around the temple and then treated us to bean-paste cakes and tea. As we all bowed and took our leave, he graciously handed each of us a slender volume of sketches of Zen temples along the Kiso.

After a long soak in a hot bath, dinner was served in the small dining room, and Mrs. Hotta served her usual spread of salmon, river fish, daikon soaked in sake, green pepper, miso soup, and plenty of beer. The first time I stayed here, over a decade ago with my wife, Emily, Mrs. Hotta had informed us that she loved the songs of Stephen Foster. The three of us had sung "Old Black Joe" and some other favorites together for over an hour, Mrs. Hotta giggling intermittently, concerned about her pronunciation. But although she does not speak English at all, her words had been perfectly clear and her voice melodious.

The Sakaju was in operation in 1880 as an inn but was a dry-goods concern long before that. In the Great Fire of 1950, it burned to the ground as did six hundred other houses. Mrs. Hotta was thirteen years old at the time of the conflagration and could see the glow from her home in a village near Mount Ontake. Later, she came to Agematsu as a bride. Now her husband had passed away, no one would follow her when she retired, and the Sakaju may close up for good, having once been considered the best inn in the area. It is hard work running an inn, even for just a few guests. There is the marketing, the cooking of meals, washing the bedding, and the general cleaning up. The master or o-kami-san is the first to rise and the last to go to bed, and when there is little or no help, this must be daunting. There is more interest in the Kiso Road these days but fewer inns, with the exception of towns like Narai, Tsumago, and Magome. We asked Mrs. Hotta how tourism could be encouraged in the less traditionally attractive towns like Agematsu and Miya no koshi, but she just answered with a wistful smile. Again, the kids move away and don't come back, and few people are interested in the intense work schedule of running an establishment like this.

It is worthwhile mentioning the delicate matter of Japanese toilets here, always a subject of concern for foreign travelers. There are, of course, still the traditional ones with just an oblong porcelain bowl almost even with the ground. The more modern of these actually have a flush mechanism, while others are simply over a deep hole in the ground lined with cement. But there are also those like the Western-style one at the Sakaju, the lid of which opens up upon entering the tiny room so that you don't have to touch it, and there is also a console that looks like it belongs in front of a pilot on a jet airplane. The buttons control (1) the up-and-down motion of the lid, (2) two types of flushing marked "large" and "small," (3) a bidet, and (4) your choice of water or hot air for "cleaning." The less adventurous can also use toilet paper. There are several other buttons on this console, but I have never been able to figure out what they are for. Nor have I asked. I have been told that there are some toilets in private homes that are connected directly to a doctor's office for urinalysis, but this may be urban legend. It is not unthinkable in this country; the ancient and modern live side by side in Japan, even on the Kiso Road.

IN THE MORNING, the three of us said our good-byes to the always-beaming Mrs. Hotta, whose head nearly touches the floor when she bows—she's less than five feet tall, so it hasn't got a long way to go. Crossing the street to the steep steps up the hill, we were back on the Kiso Road again. The narrow road led us past an elementary school and the Suo Shrine, through a residential area, across the Nakazawa Bridge, and to the small township of Mikaeri. Here is a story about this place:

> A long time ago, around the 1460s, there was a doctor by the name of Kawagoe Sankichi, who hailed from Kawagoe in the province of Musashi. He had gone to Ming China to study the art of medicine, and returned and settled in Kyoto. In his later years, however, he came to live in the Kiso and enjoyed the rest of his life here. One day, he would drop a fishing line into Nezame no toko, on another, go pick medicinal herbs in the mountains. Thus, he lived his life at leisure and at what was appropriate for himself. Three times the old man left the area, but because he was unable to forget the beauty of the natural surroundings and the easy way of life here, he came back three times as well. As the old man came back three times, the place became known as Mikaeri (三帰り), or Three Returns, but is now known by its homonym Mikaeri (見帰り), or Returning to Look.

Although Kawagoe Sankichi was an historical figure, there is a slight lack of concurrence in the recorded time period of his life (c. 1555–58) and that of the story. He may also have had something to do with the story of Urashima Taro (about whom, more to follow).

There was also a large pine tree on the land register for the old highway in the neighborhood of Mikaeri until the Meiji period, and it is said to have been there at least since the time of Old Man Sankichi. In an illustration dated 1876, it is given the name Old Man Pine and is decorated with religious ropes around its trunk. When the pine was cut down, the people in the neighborhood were concerned that something bad might happen, and sure enough, a virulent epidemic soon broke out. The people of Mikaeri quickly came together and chanted the *nembutsu*—"Hail to the Buddha Amida," a mantra of the Jodo and Jodo Shin Buddhist sects—and this was the beginning of the Mikaeri Nembutsu Association, which is still active today.

Leaving Mikaeri, we walked a short distance to a line of old wooden buildings—the Echizen-ya (famous since times past), the Tase-ya (until recently a minshuku)—with the atmosphere of the old Nakasendo. This is the upper reaches of the village of Nezame, about which an old guidebook, the *Kisoji yasumi zue,* published in 1756, simply states, "There is a stopping place called Nezame Village, famous for its buckwheat noodles." Also connected with the place is a quote from the nineteenth-century novel *Zohu hizakurige* by Ikku Jippensha. His comic antiheroes, Yaji and Kita, are on their way to Agematsu from Nojiri, and

> they reached the establishment of Nezame, where buckwheat noodles are the local famous product. There they saw a young lady at the Echizen-ya, and quipped, "More than the buckwheat noodles, the long nose hairs of the young lady will stop the traveler in his tracks."

Turning onto the street between the Echizen-ya and the Tase-ya, we descended the hill that leads down to the Rinsenji, a Zen temple established sometime around 1608 under the orders of Tokugawa Yoshinao, the ninth son of the shogun Ieyasu. In 1864, the entire temple compound except for the hall dedicated to Benzaiten burned to the ground, but was rebuilt the following year. Then, in 1971, the main temple and priests' quarters were restored, but without the architectural charm of former days. Travelers have tarried here since long ago, and during the Edo period the daimyo would stop to rest or stay overnight. There are a number of stone monuments on the temple grounds, two of which are engraved with haiku by Basho and Yokoi Yuya, memorializing their visits here.

ひる顔にひる寝しよもの床の山
I'll take an afternoon nap
among the morning glories
in the mountain bed [toko no yama].
—Basho

筏士に何をか問わん青あらし
What can it be asking
the raftsman?
The wind blowing through green leaves.
—Yuya

There is yet another, by the poet Masaoka Shiki, but this was composed as he crossed the Magome Pass, leaving the mountainous defile of the sixty-six-mile Kiso Valley. It is recorded in his *Kakehashi no ki:*

白雲や青葉若葉の三十里
White clouds!
Green leaves, young leaves,
for sixty miles.

Walking past the temple, we came to a railing overlooking the deep gorge of Nezame no Toko, one of the most arresting sights in the entire Kiso Valley. Here, the river runs through what appears to be a huge split in the granite boulders that jut up from the valley floor. Depending on the season, the current will be swift and raucous, with waves dashing against the giant rocks alongside, or silent and calm, quietly flowing through the corridor, heading down to the shallows downstream. Each of the rocks has received a name after the shape it might be compared to—the flat rock next to the Urashima Shrine, for example, is called the "Bed Rock" (床岩), while the one farther in has been named the "Lion Rock" (獅子岩). On the other side of the gorge where there are "portholes" in the cliff are the "Large Pot" (大釜) and the "Small Pot" (小釜),

and the cliff itself is called the "Folding Screen Rock" (屏風岩) and the "Seat Rock" (腰掛岩). The mountain backing the opposite shore is called Toko no yama (床の山), or "Bed Mountain."

Concerning these rocks, Ota Nanpo noted,

> There are various shapes to the rocks, with names like Elephant Rock, Chopping Block Rock, Folding Screen Rock, Lion Rock, Tatami Rock, etc. but you can't really tell the difference when you look at them. . . . On the opposite bank there are several yards of towering rocks with stunted pines. . . . The sound of water reverberates throughout the valley, and should cleanse the dust of this floating world.

As Santoka sat and pondered this scene, his thoughts were, perhaps, a little more mundane.

おべんたう食べて寝覚の床で

Chowing down
my box lunch:
Nezame no toko

Counter to what one might expect, there is no bridge across the gorge, and there is a reason for this.

> Many years ago, the people of the village discussed the matter together and, as a result, a bridge was built reaching the other bank. When the bridge was completed and the villagers went to cross it, a strange thing happened: a whirlpool opened up, and the flowing waters of the Kiso suddenly took on the reflective quality of a mirror. Looking down into the water, the people could see the terrible visage of a huge cow's head floating up to the surface, and nobody had the will to cross to the other side. After that, no one has ever wanted to build a bridge there again.

Add to this another eerie story about this otherwise stunningly beautiful scene.

The guardian spirit that lived in the depths of Nezame was offered the sacrifice of a young maiden every year by the people of that village. In the years that no sacrifice was made, the crops did not grow and nothing could be harvested. Once, the beloved daughter of an old man and wife was marked to be the victim for a certain year, and in their distress, the couple went to confer with an ascetic who lived nearby. This man advised them to fry the fetus of a wild boar into small balls, bind the balls with wisteria vines, then go fishing for this spirit in a large group. In the end, they pulled up a six-foot salamander, and as a result, the problem of a yearly sacrifice was over.

Salamander or not, Ginny and Tadashi decided to descend the long stairs down to the rocks to inspect the area more carefully. I had been here a number of times before, and, in deference to my blisters, which were beginning to complain to me again, I took a leisurely walk around the temple grounds, looking at the engraved monuments, saying a short prayer at the Inari shrine, and stopping to bravely gaze down into the shallow pool of water called the Mirror Pool. Here is one more story, many versions of which exist throughout Japan.

A long time ago, in the province of Tamba, Takeno-gun, in a place called Urashima, there lived a daimyo by the name of Mizue. The son of this lord was a young man called Taro. One day, this Taro took a small boat out into the offing to go fishing, and pulled up a large white turtle. His companion raised his oar and was about to beat the turtle to death, but Taro stopped him, and released the turtle back into the sea. They caught no fish that day, and after Taro brought the boat back to shore, he was ready to return home when a beautiful young lady came up to him, seemingly out of nowhere.

She bowed deeply and said, "I am the turtle you just released. You saved my life and I want to thank you." And with this, she accompanied Taro to the palace of the Dragon King, a land of eternal youth.

In the Dragon palace, not only the Dragon King but all of his younger princesses were waiting for Taro. With deep respect, they thanked him for saving their elder sister, and asked him to stay at his leisure.

Taro enjoyed himself so that he forgot all about the passage of time, but one day he heard a rooster crowing and remembered his hometown. Suddenly, his desire to return home was so strong that he was unable to contain himself and asked the Dragon King for permission to take his leave.

"If you return home, find that your native land has become unpleasant to you, and desire to come back here once again," the Dragon King said, "I am giving you an image of Benzaiten and a copy of the *Manposhnisho,* the Mysterious Document of Ten Thousand Jewels. But I am also giving you a jeweled hand box, which you must not open under any circumstances." And with this, the Dragon King handed over these gifts to Taro.

Taro happily mounted the dragon horses that the Dragon King now loaned him and returned to his own land.

Taro thought that only two or three years had passed, and he was sure that his parents were still strong and healthy and that the neighboring people were still working happily in the fields. But when he arrived at his hometown and looked around, to his horror, he found that he recognized no one, and that the story of Urashima Taro that these unknown people had heard was that the man had lived some three hundred years ago, had gone fishing out in the offing one day, and had never returned.

Taro was totally aghast. Opening the *Manposhinsho,* he found that it contained some instructions on how to fly, and medical advice on long life. As soon as he read through the manuscript, he began traveling throughout the provinces, going where his feet led him.

Again and again, Taro's path took him to the Nezame no toko on the Kiso Road. Captivated by the beautiful scenery of the environs, he settled down in the village of Nezame and went fishing every day at Nezame no toko. But one day he was reminded by an old man in the village of the jeweled hand box that he had been given by the Dragon King, and opened it up to show the old fellow. Suddenly a purple cloud wafted out of the box, and he immediately wasted away, turning into a three-hundred-year-old man. Everyone who witnessed this was shocked, and Taro ran to a nearby pool of water, looked at his reflection, and nearly fainted dead away. Since that time, this pool has been called the Mirror Pool (姿見の池).

After this, Taro treated people with the wonder medicine he had learned from the *Manposhinsho,* but at some point he wandered off to nobody knew where.

When the people of the village went to see what the old man might have left behind, they found that the statue of Benzaiten had been placed on the Toko no iwa. There they built a small shrine, and the temple that was built later is the current Rinsenji.

A Japanese tourist couple came up and expressed curiosity about what I was looking at in the Mirror Pool. When I responded that I was checking out my age, they gave me a blank stare, looked carefully once again into the pool, and wandered off just as Ginny and Tadashi had climbed back up, winded, from the rocks below. We once again ascended the hill up to the Echizen-ya and Tase-ya, turned right, and followed the Kiso Road through a twisting, dark wooded forest, eventually reaching the national highway and the Chuo-sen. Tucked back into the woods on our left was the Ono no taki falls, once considered one of the Eight Scenes of the Kiso. In the *Kisoji meisho zue,* there is this description, which describes its present-day appearance as well:

> Its height is about thirty feet, and it falls directly into the Kiso River. This waterfall comes through the mountain valley and falls over the rocky crags like bleached cloth. At the side, there is a statue of Fudo Myo-o.

When the postwar scholar and politician Asai Kiyoshi visited the place, he brushed this poem:

ふきおろす松の嵐も音たえて
あたりすずしき小野のたきつせ

Equal to the voice
of the storm
rushing through the pines,
the refreshing, swift flow
of Ono Falls.

And, of course, there is a story connected to this delicate spray of water and mist.

Once long ago, when the villagers of Haiwara went into the mountains to cut firewood for the winter, they encountered a beautiful princess who had fled there to escape a pursuer. The princess explained the circumstances of her flight and begged the villagers over and over again to hide her from the man who would do her harm. In the end, however, the villagers refused, fearsome of later difficulties. The princess then took out some gold coins that she had carefully carried with her and offered them to the villagers if only they would take her in. But the villagers only took the coins and, again, absolutely refused her request.

There was nothing else she could do, so the princess continued her flight up the mountain road, and hid near a nameless waterfall. The next day, she was discovered by her pursuer and, rather than be taken by the man, threw herself into the waterfall and drowned. After that, the waterfall was called the Hidden Falls.

The three of us contemplated this story, left a small offering at the statue of Fudo Myo-o, and carried on. The Kisoji was again now a sidewalk on the national highway, now a footpath through the woods, now passing by a number of old residences that would seem to have been there since Meiji times. Finally, we found a traditional noodle restaurant—the Takeshiro-ya—next to the highway and had a meal of fat udon noodles with side dishes of local vegetables served on lacquer trays. We were tired and fam- ished and, seated around a long open brazier with other guests, happily finished off a meal that has bolstered travelers for the last several hundred years.

The Kiso Road now meandered onto some smaller roads through woods and passed some old houses, and in another hour, we walked into the tiny community of Suhara. Here, I said a fond farewell to Ginny and Tadashi, who would catch the train back to Agematsu and then drive back to Ibaragi Province. They had been cheerful and informative companions on the road, and I would miss their company. "Give me a companion of my way," wrote Laurence Sterne, "be it only to mention how the shadows lengthen as the sun declines." These two had been so much more than that, but with deep bows, we went our separate ways.

COURSE TIME

13 kilometers (7.8 miles). 4 hours, 55 minutes.

10 Suhara ELEVATION 1,650 FEET

*When you arrive at your lodging, it is necessary to first ask and
confirm the directions of north, south, east, and west; and then
check out the building's construction, the location of the toilet,
and the exits and entrances both front and back. This has been
taught since ancient times. This is done in case of a nearby fire, a
thief breaking and entering, or a fight breaking out.*

*When you are in your inn and a fire breaks out nearby, get your
clothes and everything around you that's important, determine the
direction of the wind, grab your baggage, and leave. Do not worry
about unessentials.*

In such times, you do not rely on the guidance of the innkeeper.

—*Ryoko yojinshu*

GOING THROUGH SUHARA, the Kiso Road is lined here
and there with various sizes of *mizubune*—literally, "water boats,"
which are the old water troughs carved out of huge logs. Tin
ladles with two-foot-long handles are placed on the edge of these
"boats," so the traveler can slake his thirst on a hot day. As elsewhere on the Kiso, this makes water the dominant presence, with
the constant background of mountains. The Kiso River is down
the hill and running parallel to the main street of the town. Suhara
was almost entirely swept away when the river flooded in 1715
and was then moved to a higher location. In the old records, we
learn that in the fire of 1888, eighty houses burned to the ground,

145

so, while the atmosphere has changed dramatically, in the line of houses along the main road, there are still some that retain the old architectural style. Along with the *mizubune*, there are also flowing water gullies along the road and small stone monuments engraved with "water god" (水神).

It was now mid-afternoon, and I walked down the hill, over the Kiso River, and on up to the Itose minshuku, where I was greeted by the two stout o-kami-sans with a "Yaa! Yonnenburi da nee!" ("Hey now! It's been four years, hasn't it!") Soon I was shown into my spacious and clean room, with a low table, a television, and wide sliding glass doors on the north and east walls. I leaned my pack up against the closet door, drank some tea, and then headed out for a temple visit, first stopping at the local *konbini*—convenience store—for my first real cup of coffee in twenty-four hours. Then, I headed back across the river, dodged the traffic on the national highway (easier without a backpack), and went back up the hill. Once again on the Nakasendo, I turned to the right, passed a mizubune full of clear mountain water, and very soon came to the steep stone steps leading up to the Joshoji. This famous temple was founded originally in the tenth century and belonged to either the Tendai or Shingon sect but was later established as Rinzai Zen in 1387. In the *Kiso shiryaku* we read,

> According to the oral traditions of the temple monks, this temple was originally at the side of the river, but then in the eighth month of 1561, it was destroyed in a great flood. Now, the land it stood on is called Teranakajima. After that, Ishikawa Bizen no kami Mitsuyoshi moved it to the old site of Kiso Yoshinari's mansion.

The weathered stone steps leading up to the temple compound are lined with huge cedar trees, moss covering most of the area where visitors do not step. As you pass through the two-storied main gate with its thatched roof of layered cypress bark, the temple grounds open up to a white gravel courtyard thinly scattered here and there with single maple trees in full autumn colors. The wood and white plaster main hall is to the left, the head monk's residence to the right, and about thirty yards ahead, there is a bell tower backed by a hill of pines, cedar, and Japanese cypress. The head monk's wife was sitting in a tiny office to my right as I entered the grounds; I paid the small entrance fee and was wished well. Leisurely drinking in the serenity of the scene, I eventually walked over to the main hall, took off my shoes as you do in all Buddhist temples, and stepped inside. The wood floors have been polished by hundreds of years of monks and visitors, while the high beams and ceiling have been blackened by as many years of burning incense. Immediately to my left was a huge statue—perhaps eight feet tall—of Hotei, the fat, always happy Buddha of the future, carved from a single piece of wood in 1992. He was surrounded by other small statues of Hotei, and before him on a low table was a copy of the Heart Sutra, the Hannya haramita kyo, which monks, nuns, and laypeople chant every day throughout the Buddhist world. Beside it was a mantra connected with Hotei for clearing out the seven difficulties and creating the seven happinesses: "Om maitare iya sowaka."

I carefully copied this down and repeated it the recommended seven times as I walked through the temple.

The spacious interior of this temple is only matched by the garden situated just outside on the west. There is a pond, maples, and pines, of course, but it also uses the principle of shakkei, or "borrowing the scenery," behind it: in this case, the mountains of the Kiso Valley far in the distance. The entire garden, then, is not only the one planted by human hands, which is surrounded by a low-roofed mud wall, but incorporates the one provided by nature as well.

I had come to the Joshoji to see the large cast iron temple bell called the "Mahabrahman" I had read about in my 1803 guidebook. It had been engraved with a poem in Chinese, the only line of which I could understand was "I wake from my dreams to the one hundred and eight tollings of the bell." I hoped that the priest would be able to read it for me. It is hung in the low roofed tower, the bottom of the bell about head high, and according to the guidebook, it is rung in the morning and the evening, sending the "clear and melodious voice of Brahman throughout the environs." On entering the temple and paying my entrance fee, I had asked the head priest's wife about the poem, and she had brought her husband out to talk with me. Unfortunately, he had no idea, and that seemed to be that. So after walking up to examine the bell and its mysterious inscription, I was about to leave when the head priest called out the octogenarian abbot, and the two of us went back up the small hill to the tower. It had started to rain, and I was doing my best to hold an umbrella over the old fellow's head as we hurried along—a cheerful, short man in the informal full blue pants and upper garments of a Buddhist priest, completely unconcerned about getting wet. Four years ago, his father had still been alive at the great age of ninety-seven; his grandson was three and was already being taught to meditate and chant the sutras.

Sadly, he explained to me that he had never really noticed the poem until now and was so nearsighted by this time that he could not see it, but he let me hear the sound of the bell by pulling back the smooth-planed log suspended horizontally by ropes. With a "One, two, three," he swung back the heavy log and struck the huge bell, which reverberated for well over two minutes with a deep sound that seemed to penetrate even the faraway mountains. Before striking the bell, he had bowed and repeated a short chant, demonstrating his reverence for it. We listened to the last reverberations in silence, rain still lightly falling, and I accompanied him back down to the temple. On the way, he explained that the original bell had been requisitioned by the military for iron to be used in the war effort in the 1940s and that the one now hanging in the tower was cast by Katori Masahiko, a man designated as a living national treasure, in 1965. I thanked him for his kindness and, as I took my leave, noticed that he stayed at the temple entrance and bowed with a one-handed *gasshou* until I was through the gate.

Back at the Itose, I sat back on my flat cushion with a beer and watched the kendo national championships on TV. An intense young man—a sixth *dan*—won for the third time. Several times, as the TV camera swept around the formal hall, I could see my friend Jon busily working his own camera to catch all the action.

Blisters on top of blisters: how was I going to walk the next day? At last, I hobbled off to the bath, but it was a small one, and there was someone else about to go in as well. Remembering the advice from the *Ryoko yojinshu,* I told him to go ahead and to please take his time.

In the dining room, the ladies in the kitchen served up a feast of sashimi, shrimp cooked with Japanese tangerines, sukiyaki, Spanish mackerel, steamed snapper, miso soup, various local vegetables, and more, which, again, I couldn't quite finish. I did not want to be impolite and was relieved to notice that the only other guest, a fiftyish newspaper man from Tokyo, left some of his meal as well. The two of us chatted for a while, and he informed me that he was also walking, not just the Kiso Road, but the entire Nakasendo on weekends and holidays. He had already walked the Tokaido, which was quite different from the Kiso, he said, but with its own charm. Tomorrow he would return to Tokyo and back to work. We bid each other good night and returned to our rooms.

———

泊まりにてもしや近火のある時ハ立したくして次に荷をだせ
When a fire breaks out
near the place
you are staying,
first get ready to leave,
only then, think of your bags.
　　　　—*Ryoko yojinshu*

At four thirty, I was awakened by the sound of nearby small explosions. Soon there were sounds of sirens far away, coming closer and closer until they seemed right outside my sliding glass doors. More sirens, and I could see concerned-looking men in fire-man uniforms running past, and a lot of bright lights. I finally got up out from under my comfortable and warm futon and walked to the back door, where I found one of the old o-kami-sans, who was already making breakfast preparations in the kitchen. The two of us went outside to take a look. Flames and smoke were coming from a house about a hundred feet across a small field, and it didn't look good. You see the sign 火の用心—"Be careful about fire"—everywhere in Japan, and fire has been a great concern ever since ancient times. Until recently, almost all houses have been made of wood and straw-reinforced clay, and they are quick to ignite and quick to burn down. The o-kami-san and I discussed the matter a little more, mostly with expressions of sympathy for her neighbors, and, with a "Just as you'd think, you have to be careful with fire," she went back to work in the kitchen, and I to my room.

At five thirty, smoke was still rising from what was left of the neighbor's house, the flashing lights were still on, but the firemen appeared to be wrapping things up. At six, smoke was still rising but illuminated by something—more fire?—and large hoses were still laid out in front of my sliding glass doors.

After breakfast, I was apologetically questioned by a policeman as we sat at the dining table. When did you come to Japan? Where are you going? Why are you here? Do you really like the Kiso? I was the only suspicious character around, I suppose, but before long, another officer walked up and said that the source of the fire was discovered to have been a kerosene heater on the second floor. The policeman who had been questioning me as we shared tea got up with a deep bow and another apology, jotted some last things down in his notebook, and backed out of the front door. Finally, I checked out, shouldered my backpack, and was sent off with smiles and bows from the o-kami-sans, who expressed their hopes that I would be back before another four years. As I walked down the driveway past the onlookers, my policeman friend waved at me from his car with a smile; I returned the same and was off to the konbini for a hot cup of coffee.

Ready to go, I yet again hiked back up the hill to the Nakasendo. The day before, I had noticed that a shop across from the railroad station had *hanazuke*—a tea pickled with salt and cherry blossoms and a traditional famous product of Suhara—for sale. It was still early for business, and the little shop was closed, but when I knocked tentatively, a middle-aged lady with a dubious expression opened the door and asked what I wanted. I explained that, well, I was in Suhara, and I really should sample some *hanazuke*. All of her doubt then faded away; she laughed, invited me to sit down at a small table, and prepared some tea in the rear kitchen.

The tea was salty but very refreshing, and the woman looked at me out of the corner of her eye to see my reaction. *Umai!* "Delicious," I said to her apparent relief and, as further proof, bought a small package to take back home with me. We exchanged a few pleasantries as I put the package into my backpack; she walked me to the door and wished me a good trip: "Itte irasshai!" ("Go and come back again.")

Doubling back, I walked through the post town, the *mizubune* bubbling with water—someone had placed a spray of red and blue flowers in one of them—past the temple steps, and into a wooded area up a steep hill called the Nagasaka, or "Long Slope." At the top of the rise, the scenery opened up to my right with a view of the river now far down below and the beautiful ridgeline of Mount Kisokoma in the distance. Even from this high up, the river water appeared to be a clear blue green, running over thousands of huge rocks. Just beyond the river, the low mountains of the Kiso were full of drifting mists. The weather forecast early this morning had been for rain and lightning, but it was clearing up, and I was happy to think that my poncho would stay in my pack.

The road wound around the mountain, always with the river visible below, with only an occasional car passing by. In about an hour, I found the sign pointing the direction to the Iwadedera, a small but lovely old temple situated high on an overhanging rocky cliff. Stone statues of Batto Kannon and Jizo lined the long stone steps leading up to the platform jutting out from the temple entrance. The *honzon*, or object of worship, here is a Batto Kannon, the horse-headed goddess of mercy, worshipped by horse raisers from all over Japan, and a great number of votive pictures of horses are consecrated inside the temple (the wide slatted door of which was locked).

Today the maples and ginkgo trees along the platform were bursting in reds and yellows, and flanked a single green pine in their very center. The sky had cleared completely for the moment, and there was nothing to break the silence other than the current of the nearby Inagawa River, a tributary to the Kiso. I took off my pack and rested on the steps of this secluded and unattended temple for an hour. Finally, I signed the notebook register that hung from the edge of the door and tossed a few hundred yen into the offering box with prayers that I might someday come back again.

Of course, there are many tales about this temple, and this is one concerning its origin.

A long time ago, there was a very kind-hearted man who lived in this place, and who made his living by the side of a teahouse making straw sandals for travelers and straw boots for their horses.

During the winter of one year, a rather dignified traveler came riding by and, as his horse's straw boots were torn, he asked the old man to make a new set. Unfortunately, however, the old man had only enough time to fit the horse with a single boot before the traveler had to continue on his way.

The old man saw them off, but feeling sorry for the horse, hurried to finish the other boots, and went running after them. Chasing them down at the crossroads of the settlement at Ojima, he handed over the boots at once. The traveler was extremely pleased, and tried to pay the old man for his work, but the old man refused the offer, being struck by the countenance of the man. At that point, the traveler took a chip of wood, took out the brush and ink he carried at his side, and wrote *Batto Kanzeon Bosatsu.* "Believe in this," he said as he handed it over to the old man, "and you will benefit by it." He then continued on with his horse, but suddenly vanished from sight.

When returning to his house, the old man installed the chip of wood in the god shelf where it began emitting a bright light from time to time. Thinking this to be rather strange, he took the chip and hid it between some rocks at the mouth of the Inagawa River, and there it gave off more light than before.

Those people who put faith in this phenomenon saw good things happen to them, and, as rumors spread about the neighborhood, a sort of religious sect was formed.

Soon, with the efforts of the people of the surrounding area, a temple was erected where the wood chip was enshrined by itself, and a single statue of a Batto Kannon was carved and worshipped there. People continue to gather and celebrate this faith to this very day.

After crossing the Inagawa Bridge, there is the choice of taking the old Kiso Road up through the hills or walking down to the national highway with its view of the river and mountains. Years ago, my friends Robbie and Gary and I had chosen the former. The three of us had been hiking the Kiso and at this point had decided to go up rather than around. After hiking up a steep incline on that sunny day, we were pleased to find that the old road wound through gentle hills dotted here and there with small farming communities. At one of these villages, we happened on a local festival that consisted mostly of three adults—one beating a drum, one playing a flute, and the other wearing a *shishi,* or lion mask, chasing a few screaming and laughing children as they danced from door to door eliciting funds for the local temple. An elderly grinning bystander was telling me that the mask—about three times the size of a human head, painted red, yellow, and black with an open mouth and wide eyes—was quite old and valuable, when I heard some more delighted screaming and laughing. Robbie, without much pressure I'm sure, had been persuaded to put on the mask and was doing a yeoman's job of performing the dance. This made for great general merriment, but after a while we took our leave, bowed deeply, and went on our way to the sounds of the flute and drum and happy children behind us. Following the road through the hills, we passed the Tencho-in, a Zen Buddhist temple founded in 1593 but completely rebuilt in 2000. In front of the gate was a Maria Jizo or Maria Kannon—even the priest was not sure—and inside the main hall, a beautiful statue of Amida Buddha, the "Buddha of the Western Paradise." We then passed more fields and peaceful valleys, ending in an easy walk into the post town of Nojiri.

This time, however, I decided to take the less steep hill, which eventually descended to the national highway and the Kiso River. When the river came into view, I looked across to see the tile roofs of the Chokoji, an ancient temple established in 937, peeking above the tree line and thick bamboos surrounding it. In this temple are enshrined three statues of Yakushi Nyorai, the "Medicine Buddha of Emerald Light." Among the various Buddhas worshipped in Japan, Yakushi Nyorai is the healer, the "doctor of souls and bodies." He is also very compliant with the wishes of us sentient beings:

> A long time ago, people traveled the Nakasendo on horseback, but when they got as far as Sekiyama, their horses would become restive, and they would be thrown from their saddles.
>
> People thought this was rather strange, and when they investigated the matter, they could see that there was a blinding light coming from the Chokoji on the opposite bank. This light was apparently coming from the gold color of the Medicine Buddha

enshrined there and, reflecting in the eyes of the horses, had caused them to become unruly.

Thereupon, the people of the village appealed to the temple, and the Medicine Buddha granted them the favor of turning around so only his back could be seen. From that time on, it is said that no more travelers fell from their horses on this stretch of the road.

Soon I passed through the old town of Okuwa, where strings of drying orange persimmons hung from the second stories of almost every other house. In the *Ryoko yojinshu* we are advised,

> You should not wantonly stretch out your hand for fruit such as pears, persimmons, citrons, or mandarin oranges being raised at people's houses along the road or in the middle of fields, no matter how delicious they may seem. . . . If you receive complaints in an unfamiliar place, you must understand that the odds will not be in your favor.

I was reminded of an old Zen proverb,

瓜田不納履、梨下不整冠
Do not tie your shoes in a melon patch;
do not adjust your helmet under a pear tree.

and carefully looked straight ahead as I walked along. Eventually I was back onto the narrow old Kiso Road running along the river, thick with vegetation on both sides. I stopped for a local train that passed across the road and, after a slight grade, limped into the post town of Nojiri.

COURSE TIME
Suhara to Nojiri: 7 kilometers (4.2 miles). 3 hours.

不信只看八九月、紛紛黄葉満山川

You who are without faith, simply look at September, October;
The yellow leaves fall in confusion, filling the mountains and
rivers.

—Zenrin kushu

Nojiri is a typical mountain town, located on what is perhaps the broadest and deepest stretch of the Kiso River in the entire valley. The houses and shops are all relatively new due to fires in 1791, 1824, and a particularly disastrous one in 1894 when nearly half of the buildings were destroyed. Still, it was and remains a prosperous town, and in the census of 1843, it was recorded that there were 108 houses inhabited by a population of 986 people. There was also a honjin, a waki-honjin, two forwarding agents, and nineteen inns. In the heyday of the post towns, Nojiri was known for its seven bends in the roads, constructed so as to confuse any invading armies.

It was, however, not always such a pleasant place to stay over for the night. According to Ota Nanpo,

> In Nojiri, I spent the night in the *honjin* operated by Mori Shosa Hyoemon. This is a structure of wooden planking without a fence or wall. Nevertheless, I saw a placard stating that Makino Bizen no kami stayed here last year for one night on October 9th when coming on official business. It is truly a "journey" when staying in such a miserable setting. All night long there was the sound of the rain, and the rough reverberation of the flow of the river.

157

Echoing this, in the *Kisoji meisho zue,* it says,

> The flow of the Kiso River [here] booms and leaps, and sounds
> like thunder. During times of heavy rains, there is a great fear of its
> overflowing its banks.

My stay was far more enjoyable. As I walked into town, my first
stop was the Donguri Coffee Shop, where Ms. Ueda, the o-kami-
san, welcomed me with exclamations of how long it had been. I
ordered a "morning set," despite the fact that morning was over,
and she brought me a tray with coffee, yogurt with blueberry jam,
a thick slice of buttered toast, and a hard-boiled egg. We chatted
for a while, but her accent is difficult to understand—she had come
to Nojiri as a bride from another town across the mountains, Hida
Takayama. Another patron, an older gentleman from the area, also
joined the conversation. His dialect was even more foreign to me,
and I was not very talkative. When he left, however, he smiled and
quoted the old Zen and tea ceremony adage *ichigo ichie* (一期一会),
"Each meeting a once-in-a-lifetime event"—and I was ashamed of
my reticence. When I took my own leave a few minutes later, Ms.
Ueda, who had also noticed my limp, insisted on bringing me an
antibiotic cream and bandages for my feet.

It was still too early to check in to my inn, so I made my way
to the Myokakuji, a large Buddhist temple established in 1624,
on the edge of town. There is a large, beautiful garden here, with
one ancient ginkgo tree, at this time of year in full yellow autumn
array. Here and there are small stone statues of the Buddha's dis-
ciples, but most striking is the Maria Kannon. This is also carved
out of stone, stands about two and a half feet high, and has the
date 1832 inscribed on the back. At first glance, it seems to be a
Thousand-Armed Kannon (actually, there are only six arms), but
in her right hand she appears to hold something like a cross. This
again suggests that there must have been communities of "Hidden
Christians" all along the Kiso, doing their best not to be discovered but intent on worshipping their icons in one way or another.

Inside the temple is a six-foot statue of Daikoku, made from a single piece of Japanese cypress. There is also a large room filled with the mortuary tablets and black-and-white photographs of members of the community who were killed during World War II. It is moving and sad to think of the young men recruited from this mountain town—probably all farmers' sons who wanted nothing more than to till what fields were available, but who responded, as did their American counterparts, to the patriotic call of their country.

After viewing the rest of the temple—there is also a beautiful gold-leaf, foot-and-a-half-tall statue of Kannon enshrined there—the priest's octogenarian aunt, Sumiko, came out to greet me. She, too, kindly remembered my visit four years ago and invited me to stay for a cup of tea. As we talked, she told me that she had been born in Kyoto but was raised in Yamaguchi Prefecture far to the southwest. She had come to the temple, like Ms. Ueda, as a bride. Sumiko carries herself with a wonderful elegance, perhaps due to her Kyoto background, and speaks limited English but with a surprisingly good accent. We talked about my favorite poet, Santoka, and how he had walked through the Kiso in the 1930s. Like the abbot in Suhara, she saw me off at the temple gate, bowing until I was out of sight. From the steps there was a clear view of Mount Kisokoma against a bright blue sky.

With Sumiko's instructions, I walked to a konbini and asked for the whereabouts of the Kakumei Shrine nearby. The young ladies attending the store assured me that there was no such thing in these parts, and I left, but an old man I encountered on the roadside told me to take the next road up the hill though the forest. Sure enough, I turned left at the next dirt road, continued up the hill through dark cedars and cypresses, and finally found a narrow mossy path that crossed a tiny stream and led up to the shrine. The wooden building was quite old and dilapidated, surrounded by ancient trees and slippery pathways, but clearly visited from time to time: a large straw broom was hung on the wall outside for believers to sweep up after prayers. Behind the shrine there is a statue of Fudo Myo-o and some small houses for the gods—a dark and shadowy setting, appropriate for mountain worship. The story with this out-of-the-way shrine is as follows.

> Sometime between 1624 and 1644, there was an ascetic by the name of Kakumei, who frequently did religious ascetic practices at Komiya Falls. He always stopped at the Kose-ya in Nojiri, and one day he spoke to the people of the inn just before leaving for Mount Ontake.
>
> "At this time, it is my ambition to open a mountain to religious practice at Kiso Ontake. If I am able to do so, I will not be returning here again. You have always been kind to me, and I would return the favor, even if just a little, and am giving you this paper charm for safe childbirth. If the person who receives this charm does not have easy childbirth, just tear it up and throw it in the Kiso River."
>
> After this, every woman who received the charm had an easy childbirth, and the people of the area were extremely happy and thankful. Thinking it over, they felt that Kakumei's charm was not just some simple thing, and sometime during the 1850s, a number of concerned people discussed the matter, and decided to build a shrine at the Komiya Falls. There they worshipped the spirit of Kakumei, and organized the Ontake-kyo Safe Childbirth Sect. Every year on the twenty-first day of the fourth month and the twenty-third day of the tenth month festivals are held, at one time attracting over a thousand people.

I was sorry to have missed the festival by only a few days but happy to have been able to find the small shrine. Leaving a few hundred yen in the offering box in front of Fudo Myo-o, I headed back through the forest and down the hill. Once again at the konbini, I somewhat smugly showed the ladies there the photographic evidence of the shrine's existence in my camera to responses of oohs and aahs and "Who would have known?"

Now came the long walk to the Koiji minshuku, and once again, I took the wrong road. When I stopped to ask a man washing his car for directions, he declared it to be too far to walk and kindly offered to drive me there. I consulted the matter with my blistered feet for a moment, and off we went, first across the Kiso River, then the Atera River, and I was finally dropped off at the Koiji. My driver friend bowed good-bye from inside the car, and I was greeted by Ms. Uegaki Ryoko, the o-kami-san, a cheerful and talkative woman in her fifties. Ryoko quickly settled me in my room with tea, cookies, and Japanese tangerines, and it was time for a short rest.

The Koiji is a large single-story structure—originally a farm-house—situated just above some vegetable fields and overlooking the Kiso River. The two rooms designated for travelers would probably not accommodate more than four people at a time, and the toilets and sinks at the end of the hall seem to have been added for just such a number of guests. Dinners are served in the guests' rooms, but breakfast takes place at a table between the kitchen and the family's living room. This minshuku is clearly a secondary income for the family, and the traveler more or less takes part in their life—at least in the morning. It is a very comfortable setting, and Ryoko is warm and attentive, but not intrudingly so.

For travelers who wish more upscale accommodations, there is a large *onsen*, the Atera-so, just down the road, which includes some very large tile baths, a spacious dining hall, and is just across the way from a *rotenburo*, a large indoor-outdoor bath where people go to spend the day. When my wife and I stayed at the Atera-so years ago, there was a happy party taking place, celebrating the head priest's office being passed from one generation to the next. A good bit of drinking had been going on, and finally an ambulance had had to come and take someone away. The person was fine, the manager reported, and the party went on. This time, I was satisfied to be at the quiet and peaceful Koiji, looking out at the mountains from the large glass sliding door of my room.

About a ten-minute walk from the Koiji is the confluence of the Atera and Kiso Rivers. A narrow road winds up the gorge through which the Atera River flows, with steep banks and inclines on both sides, and is lined with a forest of tall, dark cypress trees, some hundreds of years old. The flow of the current is remarkably clear, the river itself being studded with thousands of stones and rocks of all sizes. Here and there are deep, still pools, reflecting the full autumn colors of the maples along the river. Although this road is not actually a part of the Kiso Road, it is not to be passed by, even if your blisters are the size of large pinto beans by this time.

So after a short rest at the Koiji, I gingerly tied on my boots and walked to the entrance of the Ateragawa Keikoku, the Ateragawa Gorge. It was about two in the afternoon, a bright sunny day, and it was nice not to be shouldering a backpack. The sides of the gorge narrow almost right at the beginning, however, and the wall-like cliffs block out all but a sliver of sky overhead. The forest is mysteriously dark, the atmosphere changes almost immediately, and the only sounds come from the current of the narrow Atera River as it rushes and vaults down to join the Kiso. The Japanese have traditionally found such places to evoke a sense of *kami,* the gods or god energy, and it is not difficult to understand why. The early inhabitants of the islands buried their dead in the mountains, and after time, the souls of the dead became resident spirits and gods. The rocks, trees, and waters of the mountains, too, were— and still are—believed to be sacred and to harbor divine spirits.

But I was not alone with the gods. After about a thirty-minute hike, there was a sign by the side of the road that warned against "bears and wasps." To my knowledge, there had been no fatal encounters on this road, and when I left the minshuku with the mention of where I was going, Ryoko simply smiled with an "Itte irasshai" ("Go and come back"). Nevertheless, now I wondered what might be looking at me through the forest as I walked on. Years ago, when I walked this road for the first time, a man pulled up in a small car, gave me two Japanese tangerines, warned me against the bears, and sped off back down the mountain. I wasn't sure what the tangerines were for, but I kept them at the ready until I was back at the minshuku. This time, to my good fortune, I had been thoughtful enough to tuck my slender volume of the *Ryoko yojinshu,* with its printed a talisman against "disasters and illnesses in the mountains and sea," into the pocket of my jacket, and thus felt assured that all would be well.

Although I had only been walking for about an hour, the light was beginning to slip away, and I started to think about turning back. On my right, however, there was a narrow mossy pathway that led to a small shrine where one might pray to the gods of the Atera. With furtive looks on either side, I made my way up the trail farther into the forest, found the old weathered wooden shrine, made a short prayer of thanks, and beat a hasty retreat to the road.

Continuing on up, I found the *ugen no taki,* or "Falls Manifested by the Rain," a thin waterfall coming over a cliff about five hundred feet up. It was almost nothing more than a feathery spray of mist, and the name indicates that it is only a true waterfall when it rains. The cliff itself is a sheer face of rock, dotted here and there by a small cypress or maple full of red, yellow, or purple leaves. Yet farther up the road were other falls and several large pools, but the light was failing quickly, and I stopped at the Tanuki Abyss—a broad, deep, and quiet pool—climbed down the boulders to cool my feet for a moment, and turned back.

Naturally enough, I had not been thinking that the hike downhill is always harder on the feet than going up, and when I finally arrived at the Kioji, I could barely walk. But as I settled into the hot bath, I felt no regrets and considered myself lucky that I had been able to take this pilgrimage again. Back in my room, Ryoko delivered a sumptuous Kiso dinner, and later, when I crawled under my futon, I drifted off feeling confident that on the next day my feet would be absolutely fine.

THE NEXT MORNING, of course, my feet were not absolutely fine, and as I hobbled into the dining room, Ryoko looked at me with some concern. Saving me the humiliation, she called up the master of my next stop, the Yakiyama no Yu, and without my having to ask, told him to meet me at the train station in Nojiri and to then drive me on up to his minshuku. I was grateful for her kindness, remembering yet again the *I-Ching* hexagram I had thrown while still back home in Florida,

> When it is time to stop, he stops; when it is time to move, he moves.

And I silently sat down to a breakfast of grilled salmon, tiny deep-fried fish in a small celadon bowl, a tomato, broccoli, small clams boiled in sugar and soy sauce, miso soup, rice, and plenty of coffee. In the adjoining room, Ryoko, her husband, her elderly mother, and her (Ryoko's) two-year-old granddaughter were enjoying a children's show on the TV, the granddaughter dancing around in front of the screen. Soon, the show was over, and the little one was taken off, reluctantly on her part, to a nearby nursery school.

The Chinese characters for Atera, 阿寺, mean, inversely, the temple of Ah, which is the first letter of the Sanskrit alphabet. According to William Soothill's *A Dictionary of Chinese Buddhist Terms,*

> [阿] is the first letter of the Sanskrit Siddham alphabet. . . . From it are supposed to be born all the other letters, and it is the first sound uttered by the human mouth. It has therefore numerous mystical indications. Being also a negation, it symbolizes the unproduced, the impermanent, the immaterial; but it is employed in many ways indicative of the positive. Amongst other uses it indicates Amitabha [the Buddha of the Western Paradise], from the first syllable in that name. It is much in use for esoteric purposes.

This character is important in the Shingon sect, an esoteric sect of Buddhism brought from China to Japan by Kukai in 806, almost four hundred years before the advent of Zen. Kukai taught that the esoteric meanings of Shingon could be conveyed not in wordy explanations, but rather through art; and one of his practices was to meditate on the character 阿, either while gazing at an artistic representation on a scroll in front of the practitioner or by visualization.

At the breakfast table, when I asked if there was such a Shingon temple in the area, the grandmother mentioned that *her* grandfather once said that there had been a temple not far from here, but nothing remained of it even when he was a boy. Ryoko's husband then interjected that that the temple had in fact been called the Andera, and that it was somehow connected with the Ainu, the people who predated the Japanese on the islands and whose ancient sites are scattered all along the Kiso. But the Ainu were, and still are, bear worshippers and would have never been exposed to Shingon at their early dates. Nevertheless, there is a strong connection with Shingon and the avatar Fudo Myo-o, who is sometimes conflated with a bear image. And what about that sign urging me to beware of bears? It seemed clear that the mystery of this place was not to be understood by reason alone. Kukai, bears, the Ainu, and the 阿 character—all pieces of a puzzle that could only be walked through, letting reason follow its own path.

After breakfast, I limped back to my room and studied the map. There seem to be three ways one could take to the next post town, Midono. The first is the Kiso Road that follows the river—and consequently the national highway and the Chuo-sen. This is a longish but direct route and may be the one—the road has changed over the years—that Kaibara Ekiken wrote of in his journal, *Kisoji*.

Generally speaking, the Shinano Road [here, the Kiso Road] runs entirely through the mountains. Particularly in the mountains of the Kiso there are distant mountains and deep valleys, and many trails that go along the edge of the slopes. The road between Nojiri and Midono is especially dangerous. In this area, the mountain is to your left, and along its side a scant stone road. On your right there are high cliffs, in many places looking like standing folding screens. Down below, the deep waters of the Kiso River, along which are many suspension bridges. . . . These are not bridges suspended across the river, but rather [go along the side of the cliffs] where the road has given out. You see a lot of these in Chinese paintings, but in other countries they are quite rare. Many wind around the slopes and promontories of the mountains, enter valleys, and again snake their way around the mountains. They are extraordinarily dangerous.

I recalled taking this road four years earlier; there had been some very steep climbing, and the only other hiker I saw had been holding his chest as though he were about to have a heart attack. Still, it had followed the Kiso River for the most part, and there had seemed to be more than the usual number of huge boulders and rocks midstream. It had been an exhausting but exhilarating walk. At the confluence of the Yogawa and Kiso Rivers, not far from Midono, there still stands a six-foot stone statue of Jizo standing on a lotus platform, placed there in 1845. The year before, on the seventeenth day of 1844, the moorland below the mountains to the east was flooded from the waters of the Yogawa, running through land that had been deforested by a lumber project of the Owari fief. Over a hundred day laborers lost their lives that day in just moments, and in the nearby villages, the event is still explained in this way.

> The Yogawa River flows down from the mountains not too far from the village of Nagiso. Many years ago, an aristocrat's house was to be built upstream in those mountains, and a large number of woodcutters was gathered under an organizing official to cut down the many trees needed for the project. Among these woodcutters was an honest man by the name of Yohei.
>
> One night during a violent rain, Yohei was awakened by the sound of someone knocking at the door of his hut. When he cautiously opened the door, he found a woman dressed in white standing sadly before him. The woman then told him that if they cut down any more trees, some terrible event would occur.

The following morning, Yohei told his colleagues about this, and they all were quite frightened and refused to continue their work. The official, however, would not hear of this and commanded them to carry on. In the end, Yohei was so frightened that he made up an excuse about having a stomach ache and left the jobsite.

At some point that night, the woman again appeared and said, "Tomorrow it will begin to rain. Please flee to the top of the mountain." She then disappeared into the darkness.

The next day, just as the woman had said, it began to rain in sheets, the earth and sand began to loosen and crumble, and the houses in the village were swept entirely away. Even parts of the Nakasendo gave way and collapsed. As this was happening, Yohei saw a white snake flowing along with the earth and sand, and understood that this snake had only taken on the form of a woman in order to warn him of the coming disaster.

After this event, Yohei quit his job as a woodcutter and took up leading packhorses loaded with foodstuffs from the province of Owari.

A statue of Jizo had been a memorial to these workers and is still prayed to in their memory; the forests have been replanted, however, and in the peaceful and quiet mountains, nothing else is left to remind us of this sad calamity.

The second path is marked the Yogawa Road on the map and leads deep inland from the river. This is a winding forested road that eventually leads back to the Kiso Road near Midono. A little more than halfway along—Ryoko informed me that the entire route takes about four hours—the traveler reaches the site of the famous Koten-an. According to tradition, this was a small hut where a Buddhist priest, a descendant of the Kiso clan, practiced his religion, and it has been well-known since ancient times for its connection with the moon. In the middle of the Edo period, Matsudaira Kunzan, the magistrate of documents for the Owari fief, made this entry in his *Poems in Chinese and Japanese of the Eight Views of the Kiso Road.*

The mist flows over the river, and the moon at midnight
Shines on the autumn scenery with the radiance of jewels.
As though answering this, my hempen robe flinches with cold;
In the mountain villages here and there, you hear the voice
of the fulling block.

Sometime between 1744 and 1748, the poet Yokoi Yuya wrote in his *Kisoji kiko,*

秋深き
高根のしけみ
分すきて
与川にすめる
月ぞ隅なき

Deep autumn:
passing through the heavy growth
of the many high peaks.
Cleansed by the Yogawa
the perfectly clear moon.

And an unknown poet wrote,

のがれきて
すまばやここに
有明の
与川の月の
ながめことなり

Fleeing to this place,
should I stay here for a while
at dawn
the Yogawa moon
will be my view.

The Yogawa Road has been designated a "historical road" and was traveled as early as 708. On this trip, it would have to be left to my imagination or to another day.

The third route can be taken directly from the Koiji minshuku. It is a tough, steep climb up through the Kakizore Gorge, peaking more or less at the Yakiyama no Yu, an onsen run by a Mr. and Mrs. Ichikawa (no relation to my friend). From the onsen, the road is all downhill, meeting the old Nakasendo, the national highway, and the Chuo-sen about halfway to Midono. This is the route I would take today, with the help of Ryoko and Mr. Ichikawa, and with no help from my feet.

About nine o'clock, Ryoko drove me across the river and to the railroad station, where I was soon picked up by Mr. Ichikawa, who smiled and said, "O-hisashiburi, desu ne." ("It's been a long time, hasn't it.") Twelve years—much too long, I thought.

For now, Ichikawa-san carefully drove his small, white truck up the narrow road that had once been a narrow-gauge railroad, used for taking lumber out of the area. We twisted back and forth up and up the steep pass, and I was beginning to feel grateful for the blistered feet that had saved me from this walk. Pulling over at the top of the pass, my driver showed me a shrine to Kannon, a small rest house for hikers, and an old stone monument engraved with the *dosojin*, the old man and woman gods that look out for travelers along the way. Finally, we climbed to a lookout from where we could see Mount Kisokoma (a mountain I had climbed with my friend Ichikawa back in 1968) and the ridgeline of the Southern Alps. It was a cloudless clear day, and we lingered for a while at the lookout, reluctant to leave.

The Yakiyama no Yu is built on a narrow plateau not far down from the pass and close enough to the Koiji River that guests can hear the voice of its currents at all times, night and day. The building is a two-story structure, part of it quite old, but my room, through the large sliding window of which I could see the autumn mountains and hear the sound of the river, was spacious and clean.

A low table had been placed in the center of the room, set with tea and soba crackers. This would be a good place to rehabilitate, I thought. It would also be the first time my jacket, which I now hung on a peg on the wall, had not been soaked through with sweat.

The onsen itself had been given a traditional look—unglazed high-fired pots with arrangements of mountain flowers, a table in the middle of the sitting room with smooth tree stumps for chairs around a rectangular open brazier filled with charcoal and ashes. Suspended from the low ceiling over the brazier was a cast-iron soot-blackened tea kettle, from which came a steady stream of steam. Just beyond the brazier was the entrance to the baths—one for men, one for women—open 24/7, which looked out to the mountains and river through large sliding glass windows. Everything was made of wood—wooden stools, wooden buckets, wooden floor and walls, and the wooden sunken baths themselves. Supplied for the bather were dispensers of body soap, shampoo, and conditioner. Santoka would have loved this place, but Ichikawa-san assured me that, to his knowledge, the poet had never come this far off the Kiso Road.

It was still a little early, so after the tea and soba crackers, I decided to take a short tour around the area. Walking down the path from the entrance, I found a soba shop, a two-hundred-year-old folk-style house that had been moved up to this place from the Yokawa area for preservation. In front of the old shop was a deep pond, in which orange and white spotted carp appeared momentarily at the surface and then disappeared. Farther along the path, through the woods, there were two little wooden outhouses for urgent use: "urgent" because these were the traditional porcelain-lined hole on the floor over which a person squats. They were neat and clean and even had a supply of toilet paper but were likely not so inviting to foreigners or to the modern urban Japanese.

Passing these by, I crossed a very shaky plank kakehashi over the river. This one was suspended by thin wire cables, and I was reminded of all the poets who had been made queasy at the very sight of such "bridges." The air was full of yellow butterflies.

Walking back to the Yakiyama no Yu, I found that Mrs. Ichikawa, a pleasant-looking woman in her mid-fifties, was cooking up my lunch in the kitchen. Her left arm had been stricken with paralysis, and she had been "sick," as she said, when Gary, Robbie, and I had been here before. She had now, however, fought her way back to doing much of the work at the onsen. I sat back at the brazier and was soon served a large, wooden lacquer bowl of ramen, filled with slices of pork, seaweed, *kamaboko* (a kind of congealed boiled fish paste—very tasty), and pickled bracken. It was hot and good and came with a large wooden spoon to finish off the broth.

After lunch, during which I was joined by two elderly hikers "just passing through," I decided on a quick nap. Kaibara Ekiken, who passed through here in the late 1600s, advised us never to sleep after a meal—it stagnates our *ch'i*—but the combination of the hot soba, cool air, and the relaxed ambiance of the Yakiyama no Yu made it hard to resist, and, gazing at the wall of autumn leaves on the mountains and listening to the sound of the river, I slipped away . . .

渓声便是広長舌、山色豊非清浄身

The valley stream is exactly the wide, long tongue [of the Buddha]
The mountain scenery is his body of purity.

I woke to the sound of Mrs. Ichikawa knocking at my door. She apologized for bothering me but suggested that I go ahead and take a bath before dinner, although I was welcome to bathe as many times as I liked. I reminded myself that this was a recuperation day, thanked Mrs. Ichikawa, grabbed the small thin towel provided by the onsen, and went down to the baths on the first floor. After disrobing, I entered the bathroom to find that another guest was already sitting in the sunken wooden tub, his wife being over on the women's side. I asked if I might join him, and he readily assented. I first washed and rinsed off and then stepped into the tub—no more than two people could fit comfortably in this one. We talked, enjoyed our soak, and looked out at the mountain. He and his wife were from a town near Nagoya and had driven out for the day to see the autumn foliage. He noted that the two other places famous for the autumn leaves were closed to cars due to landslides caused by the typhoons—a disappointment as his vacations from work were rare. We left together, wishing each other a safe trip.

Among the different types of Japanese baths, this kind is my own personal favorite. The one at the Komao had been big—enough for six people at least—but was made of tile and in an enclosed room. It was comfortable to be sure, but these rustic baths of wood and outdoor scenery cannot be compared with.

Back up in my room, I read some more from Confucius, listened to the sound of the river, and came across this passage.

子在川上曰、逝者如斯夫、夫舎昼夜

The Master was standing by the river and said, "It goes on like this, never stopping day or night."

On this evening it was quiet at the Yakiyama no Yu, and I was the only guest staying over. Ichikawa-san informed me that the next day, however, they would have about twenty guests—a full house—and this had been the situation when Robbie, Gary, and I stopped here years ago. We slept in one of the outbuildings at that time but came in to the main hall for dinner with everyone else. The place had been packed, and we all sat at low tables and were served by a number of helpers. After about an hour of great eating, the three of us were approached by a tall, slender man with a full shock of gray hair who had been seated at the table next to ours. He had been doing some pretty good damage on the sake but politely introduced himself as Mr. Yamamoto Ichiro. He was there, he explained, with his friend, a Mr. Ito, and their wives.

All of them were in their eighties and were celebrating something I never quite understood. Both men had fought in World War II with the Japanese Navy in Singapore and Burma, and when Japan surrendered, they had handed over their weapons and uniforms and were sent home. Mr. Yamamoto had been a mountain climber and snow skier in his youth and still took to the mountains whenever he could. As he had had little intercourse with Americans ever since the war, he wanted to further celebrate the occasion by introducing the three of us to *kotsuzake*, which, he said, was sake in a long dish containing *iwana*, a river fish—a method said to kill the bad taste of low-grade alcohol. A couple of cups of *kotsuzake* was quite enough, thank you, so we moved on to the better stuff for the rest of the meal. As time (and sake) went on, Mr. Yamamoto became more and more enthusiastic about his new friends and wanted to take a commemorative photo. An amateur photographer, he had all of his equipment there and set his camera up on a tripod directly in front of us. As he tried to position his tripod lower and lower, he widened his stance and lowered his hips for balance. Gradually, it became apparent that he was wearing nothing underneath his *yukata*, the thin cotton bathrobe the Japanese often wear after a bath. As he sank lower and lower, the four middle-aged high school teachers (all of them women) sitting next to us and in full view of Mr. Yamamoto's imminent full exposure were turning red and laughing. The men's wives were yelling at him to stand up straight, but he wasn't getting it and waved them off, while Mr. Ito, of course, was encouraging his friend to get just a little lower. In the end, Yamamoto-san got his photograph, and everyone else got an eyeful, but after that there was a lot more sake and laughing. Bowing deeply, the two men, now flushed quite red in the face, were led off by their wives to bed, no doubt to face a real talking to in the morning.

When I came down to the dining room this evening, Mrs. Ichikawa was waiting for me with sake and served me *iwana*, vegetable tempura, *shoyu no moto,* and huge clusters of fresh mushrooms—both shiitake and *maetake*—which she herself grilled on a small brazier on the table. She talked a lot—about her paralysis and how she had overcome her depression and immobility through will power and knowing that only she could do it. Her calligraphy, which she practiced in order to regain coordination, was hung here and there in the inn. Her style was *kuzuji*, or "broken characters," perhaps not on purpose, but which had a lot of charm and was quite whimsical and captivating. When Gary, Robbie, and I were here so many years ago, she had been in bed and couldn't or wouldn't come out, and Mr. Ichikawa had had to run the whole show. It must have been doubly hard on him, and I remember his being rather taciturn at the time—quite unlike the way he was now.

Mrs. Ichikawa and I continued to talk and sip sake long after I could eat no more, but I finally excused myself to go upstairs to my room. She invited me to have another bath, but I would have probably sunk to the bottom. In my room, I read folktales of the Kiso for a while until I could keep my eyes open no longer. Spreading out the futon, I fell asleep to the now familiar sound of the Koiji River.

夜をこめて水が流れる秋の宿

Water flowing
into the night:
the autumn inn.
                              —Santoka

AT FOUR THIRTY, I was awakened in the dark by two competing roosters, one crowing immediately after the other, and was entertaining some very un-Buddhist thoughts about them as I tried to get back to sleep. At six thirty, they gave up, and so did I. Although ready for coffee, I was aware that they slept late here because of Mrs. Ichikawa's condition and so settled in to enjoy the early-morning light from the warmth of my futon. The weather was cold and clear. It was extremely quiet here in the mountains—other than the roosters and the river—and I was beginning to miss the human company that a lonely night at the Yakiyama no Yu had lacked. I would soon have enough of that in the next two towns of Tsumago and Magome.

It was cold even inside the onsen, but after a while I trotted downstairs, announced my presence with an *ohayoo*—good morning!—and waited patiently by the now-cold brazier. Mrs. Ichikawa presently appeared with a small cup of coffee and a big smile. Her paralysis seemed to be a little worse in the morning, but she worked gamely away and always in good cheer. Sometime during the night, she had hung a piece of her calligraphy, 夢, "dream," in the dining room, and in the hallway leading to my room, one brushed with 一雨千山潤, "A single rain benefits a thousand mountains," both with messages for herself and others, I presume. Then, breakfast was served: two kinds of daikon, miso soup, rice with a raw egg and seaweed strips, grilled mushrooms, sliced turnip dipped in olive oil and black pepper, and chopped lettuce—not your ordinary fare, but one to start the day off well.

Well fed if not well slept, I returned to my room, adjusted my still-full pack, and headed downstairs to check out. As I was about to go out through the front entrance, I made the mistake of admiring a small piece of unglazed pottery meant to hold a single flower. Before I knew it, it was wrapped up along with a small similarly unglazed cup and given to me as a souvenir. Protests did no good, and I found myself trying to fit the package containing the two fragile items in between my socks and underwear, adding a short prayer that the contents would remain safe for the rest of the trip. I should have known better by this time—express admiration for something in this country and it will soon be yours. Lack of attachment is a hard lesson to learn but one taught by Buddhism in Japan for over a thousand years.

Outside, I waited for Mr. Ichikawa to take me down the

mountain to the next post town, but there he was bowing deeply at the entranceway. Then, Mrs. Ichikawa drove up in a small white car, and I realized that *she* would be doing the driving. I put my backpack in the backseat and hopped in the front, trying not to show any concern, and off we went. We chatted all the way down the mountain, and she explained how living in the countryside with limited mobility had been terrible. She had forced herself to relearn how to drive, she explained, but with her right hand and foot only. Down we went, around sharp curves and narrow one-way roads, and she handled the standard shift like a race-car driver. Arriving in front of the railroad station at Nagiso, she gave me a big hug—not the usual good-bye in Japan. I hugged her back and gave her a kiss on the cheek, and there were tears in her eyes.

I bowed low until she drove out of the parking lot and disappeared back onto the highway.

COURSE TIME
Nojiri-shuku to Midono-shuku: 10 kilometers (6 miles). 3 hours, 20 minutes.

12 Midono

*There is something to be learned from a rainstorm. When
meeting with a summer shower, you try not to get wet and run
quickly along the road. But doing such things as passing under
the eaves of houses, you still get wet. When you are resolved from
the beginning, you will not be perplexed, though you still get the
same soaking. This understanding extends to everything.*

—Hagakure

THE LATE-SEVENTEENTH-CENTURY *Kiso kaido yadotsuke*
describes Midono as "a poor-looking post town"; a hundred years
later, Ota Nanbo called it "a wretched place"; and as late as the
1970s, the *Konjaku nakasendo hitori annai* notes that it is nothing
more than "a quiet line of shops separated from the national highway." Okada Zenkuro, however, saw the town in a different light.

This post town has many rice and vegetable fields, and is situated
on both sides of the Kiso River. It is better established than the
post town of Tsumago. . . . Among the leaders of the town are men
of considerable high character, and when bad years come, they
provide aid to those of the lower classes. This is, indeed, com-
mendable. About forty-six or forty-seven men go out for lumber
work on a daily basis.

Near the entrance to the town is a stone marker memorializing
the emperor Meiji's having passed through, but on the site of the

honjin, which was destroyed in a large fire in 1881, is now a two-story building connected to the publishing business. An ancient weeping cherry tree, once part of the honjin's garden, remains on the spot. With a trunk of five feet in circumference and twenty-four feet high, it must be a magnificent sight when it blooms in the spring. Not one inn remains in the town, so the traveler must take note of what is there and move on.

In Midono, however, is one of the most interesting displays on the Kiso Road. A short walk back north and up the hill from the train station is the Tokakuji, a temple now operated as a Soto Zen temple but that was originally established in 729, long before either Zen or esoteric Buddhism had been brought to Japan. Years ago, when my friends Robbie and Gary and I dropped through, the priest had invited us in for tea and showed us a three-and-a-half-foot-long gong he used as the temple "bell." This had been made by an American friend out of a laughing-gas canister cut off at the bottom, suspended by a chain from the side of the temple, and was to be struck—the priest demonstrated this enthusiastically—with a baseball stuffed inside a sock. He then showed us the temple's true treasure—one that attracts a number of visitors to this out-of-the-way place—a large collection of statues carved by the eccentric seventeenth-century Shingon Buddhist priest, Enku (1632–95).

Enku carved his statues of Buddhist deities and Shinto gods with a small hatchet, from almost any piece of wood he could find, from rotten driftwood to tree trunks. Contrary to almost all other Buddhist statuary, his pieces are full of a strange energy and could be called "primitive," although that does not do justice to them. When I showed photos of them to a sculptor friend of mine in Miami, he could not believe that they were from the seventeenth century and said that they looked more like something influenced by Picasso. Here is a description of Enku from the late-eighteenth-century *Kinsei kijin den zoku kinsei kijin den* (Eccentrics of Recent Times).

The monk Enku was from a place called Takegahana in the province of Mino. He left home to become a monk when young, and stayed at one temple or another, but when he was twenty-three, left, and ensconced himself on Mt. Fuji and again on Mt. Haku in Kaga. One night, the avatar of Mt. Haku appeared to him and instructed him to repair the Miroku Temple at Ikejiri in the province of Mino. He accomplished this quickly, but did not stop there, and went on to the Zenkoji Temple at Mt. Kesa in Hida. . . .

Enku carried only a single hatchet, and with this went about carving Buddhist statues. At Mt. Kesa he carved statues of the Two Guardian Kings on withered trees that were still standing. When you look at these even now, you may wonder if they are not like the works of the Buddha.

Enku knew if a person was coming. Also, he could look at a person or a house and tell if they would last for a long time or soon decline. He was never mistaken.

One time, he passed by the residential castle of Lord Kanamori in Takayama of this province, and remarked that the castle had no *ch'i*, or energy. Sure enough, in one or two years the lord was transferred to Dewa, and, except for the exterior citadel, the castle fell into ruins.

Again, the guardian spirit of Onyu Pond was seizing people, so that no one would walk by the pond alone or even when accompanied by someone else. Enku took a look, and stirred up the water. Finding that there was something suspicious about the matter, he declared that there was going to be some disaster in the province. Since the people knew that there had been something strange about the place from the very beginning, they were quite alarmed, and begged him to help them from this misfortune. In short order, Enku took up his hatchet, carved a thousand Buddhist statues in just a few days, and sank them to the bottom of the pond. After that, no one was ever seized again by the guardian of the pond, even while walking there alone.

Enku then traveled east of Hida and into the country of Ezo

[Hokkaido]. No one there knew about the Buddhist Way, so he explained the Dharma and converted many people. Even today, he is referred to as a present-day Buddha, and his light lingers there in deep respect.

Later, Enku returned to Ikejiri in Mino Province, and finished his days there. In the provinces of Mino and Hida, he became known as the Saint of the Cavern because he lived in a cave.

Enku seems to have been a practitioner of Shugendo and joined small groups of *yamabushi* at Mount Ibuki, a bleak mountain visible from the bullet train when traveling between Nagoya and Kyoto. He also climbed two unexplored mountains in the northern island of Hokkaido to set up Shugendo practice there. At some point he vowed to carve 120,000 statues, and by all accounts he was able to accomplish this promise. He left many of these carvings throughout the Kiso Valley, and some are still owned by private individuals whose ancestors had received them in return for some kindness shown to the old priest.

Enku passed away on the fifteenth day of the seventh month, the day of the Bon Festival, a festival of the dead. According to tradition, he requested that a hole be dug in the ground near the bank of the Nagara River, and when this was completed, he sat down in the hole and had himself covered up. Breathing through a bamboo tube, he chanted sutras and rang a small bell until he finally passed away. His grave marker may be found at the Mirokuji, a temple in the Ikejiri section of Seki City.

On the way to the Tokakuji, I encountered three middle-aged Japanese women hikers from Tokyo who had just passed by the temple as they walked this section of the Nakasendo. They had not known that the Enku statues are enshrined there and decided to join me to take a look. The temple today is a large wooden structure with a roof of stone tiles and a gravel foreyard, and it appears to have undergone a good bit of repair since I visited it last. Alas, the laughing-gas "bell" is no longer there or has been moved to a less visible spot.

We rang the bell at the priest's residence, but there was no answer—both the priest and his wife were away—so I guided the ladies to the small shrine where some of Enku's finger- and hand-sized statues of the "Seven Happy Gods" are kept in a glass-encased safe. Such secure measures were not always taken here, but as I was adjusting my backpack straps at the train station earlier in the morning, the station master informed me that a number of these priceless treasures had been stolen from the shrine some years ago.

Even with their small size and position behind a heavily locked glass case, these tiny statues radiate energy and life, and we stood gazing silently at them for some time. Carefully inserting some coins in the offering box, we then bowed low to the shrine and walked away. The ladies had decided that they would stay and look around the temple, but the sky was beginning to darken with purple clouds, so I bid good-bye and hastened on my way.

The Kiso Road now follows a winding path through rice and vegetable fields and behind some residential backyards. I crossed a bridge over a small river—a stream, really—with the interesting name of Januke 蛇抜け. This is literally "pulling out the snakes," and as often, when I asked people on the way what this meant, I got a number of different answers. The two I liked best were (1) that the river winds back and forth like a snake, and (2) there was an earthquake here once, and with the trembling of the earth, all the snakes came out along this stream. I was left to take my pick.

Not long after crossing the Januke River, I found myself climbing up the slope of the little neighborhood of Wago. In the *Kisoji meisho zue,* the text notes,

> The famous local product here is Wago sake. Many years ago, there was no sake in the Kiso Valley, so the villagers of Wago set out to

produce some. It is made from the water of the valley and has a light taste. You will like it.

And, in the *Jinjutsu kiko,* Nanpo describes it this way.

> Seeing the placard that advertised "Wago Quality Sake," suspended from a man's house in a village called Wago, I stopped my palanquin momentarily and, taking a breather, thought I would have a taste of this so-named "quality sake." It was in no way inferior to the Ch'u mi-ch'ung of Yunnan [a southern region of China]. When I asked the proprietor of the place about this, he said that they brewed it from the pure waters of this valley. Combine this sake with the mochi I had tasted previously, and you have a double uniqueness. This is not in the category of finding something to be delicious when you're starving, or thinking something to be satisfying when you're dying of thirst.

Unfortunately, sake is no longer brewed in Wago, so, unlike Nanpo, I had to walk on. And it had started to rain. Though it was mostly uphill, the mists and clouds were moving between the mountains like something you would see in a Chinese painting. I was soaked, regardless of the small umbrella I had been thoughtful enough to buy in Nagiso, and suspected that I did not present a very dashing figure.

> うしろすがたのしぐれてゆくか
> Seen from behind
> as I go:
> soaked to the skin?
> —Santoka

For a while the path went downhill, but then up once again and I ascended the Godozaka, or "Godo Slope." Godo is another small village on the Nakasendo, now mostly new houses, and probably a bed town for people working in Tsumago or elsewhere.

Again, Ota Nanpo:

> There is a stopping place called Godo, consisting of just two or three human habitations. A placard there announces that the local famous products are bean-jam buns and bean-jam rice cakes. I tried out the rice cakes, and they were just as good as anything in the capital. I thought that even on the Tokaido, rice cakes like this are probably rare.

At the top of the slope, surrounded by a small woods, is a shrine dedicated to Kabuto Kannon, or the "Helmet Kannon." It was here that Yoshinaka had had a small temple built sometime between 1177 and 1181 when he was constructing a castle to the south just outside of Tsumago. The temple was to protect the castle from the northeast direction, considered to be unlucky and an entranceway for demons. At some point, Yoshinaka took off his helmet and had the small statue of the Horse-Headed Kannon removed from its crown and installed inside a Buddhist statue carved by the monk Gyogi (670–749). I later learned that this statue, too, had recently been stolen but replaced through donations made by the good people of Godo. At a later date, the ceiling of the shrine had been painted with illustrations of fanciful plants and animals in colorful ten-inch squares by the famous Kano Eitoku (1543–90). In the very center, directly over the current statue, is a circle surrounding a single Sanskrit syllable, indicating that this is perhaps a temple connected to the Shingon or Tendai sect. But this is a quiet, mostly unvisited place, and there was no one here to inform me.

Back on my way, the rain had let up, in a few yards the road split, and the old Kiso Road veered off to the right through some low, but well-defined mountains. In a little over a quarter mile, the path went up the mountain on the right, to the old Tsumago Castle. Tired and wet, I decided that it was worth the climb.

Years ago, my wife and I had heard monkeys crying deep in these mountains, but on this day there was nothing but the sound of the light rain. The climb up is a stiff one but well marked. Here and there are ditches—the signs say "moats"—which must have been meant to slow down the enemy, even if just a little. Huge cedar and cypress trees are all about, which, with the steep climb, would also have impeded attackers, but given them some cover at the same time. At the top of the mountain, nothing remains but a grassy area where the castle might have been. During pre-Edo periods, however, the mountains themselves were considered "castles," so perhaps there should be no surprise about the lack of ruins. Otherwise, there are only a few large stone monuments, some inscribed with archaic characters I could not read, others illegible with age and covered with lichens.

夏草や兵共がゆめの跡
Summer grasses:
all that remain
of the warriors' dreams.
—Basho

At the southern edge of this tiny plateau is a good view of the post town of Tsumago. On the northern edge, an unwalled, open rest house where trekkers can sleep offers a good place to rest. The rain had momentarily stopped, and the clouds and mists still moved across the mountains across the valley. There are many battles associated with Tsumago Castle, and here is one as related in the guidebook *Kiso: Rekishi to minzoku wo tazunete*.

> In the spring of 1584, Hideyoshi was worried that Ieyasu would attack him as he moved down toward the capital, and so ordered Kiso Yoshimasa to block the Kiso Road and to rebuild the castle at Tsumago. Yoshimasa then entrusted Yamamura Yoshikatsu with a force of three hundred mounted samurai. The castle was surrounded on four sides by high mountains, the area was thick with oaks and pines, and below it flowed the Kiso River. Thus, it was a position of strategic importance.

Ieyasu ordered his general Suganuma Sadatoshi to lead more than seven thousand horsemen to make an attack on the castle. When the attacking force raised a triumphal song, those within the castle also put their voices together, but discharged only a few fire-arms. Witnessing such a weak resistance, Suganuma's men thought there could only be a small force inside the castle, and so climbed the mountain to make their attack. At this point, huge logs and boulders were thrown down on them, and this was accompanied by a thick rain of bullets. Unable to continue the attack, the army retreated, surrounded the castle, and spent some days in waiting.

At this point, some soldiers from Oshima arrived, formed an alliance with the attackers, and further blocked the surrounding roads. Thus, inside the castle, the situation became critical: munitions and other supplies decreased day by day. Moreover, the villagers of nearby Yamaguchi colluded with the enemy, dammed up the water supply, and were about to lead the attackers into the castle. Mori Tadamasa, the general in charge of Kaneyama Castle in the neighboring province of Mino, was alarmed when he was informed of these developments and, as an ally of the Kiso, offered to come to the castle's aid. Yoshikatsu, however, simply tightened his defenses and refused any help.

Nevertheless, their supply of gunpowder eventually ran out, and there was nothing they could do. At this point, however, Ko'ichizaemon stole out of the castle in the middle of the night, and ran down to the Kiso River behind the enemy lines. There, at a place called Uchigafuchi, the river's current was as swift as an arrow, and with the green color of the water, you could not guess its depth. Ko'ichizaemon took off all of his clothes, swam to the opposite side, and then hurried along the bank to Midono, where an allied force was encamped. Once there, he explained the castle's dire situation in detail. Thereupon, thirty men who were experts in the way of the river tied up bags of gunpowder into their hair, crossed the river, and entered the castle. Yoshikatsu was overjoyed, and at dawn fired off a volley of two or three hundred rounds, immediately felling twenty or thirty horsemen. The attackers, of course, were alarmed, thinking that reinforcements had somehow arrived.

Now, in cooperation with the villagers of Yogawa, the monks that resided at the Koten-an climbed up to the peak of Mount Shiba with a great number of paper flags, planting them here and there, and as night fell, lit watch fires throughout the mountain. The flames lit up the night sky, and the enemy thought that surely Hideyoshi's reinforcements had come from Fukushima, and that they were surrounded on two sides. Seeing this, Yoshikatsu had his soldiers steal the march on the enemy by having them lie in wait at the Araragi mountain road, and then dispatched yet other troops, sending the enemy into a chaotic retreat. Needless to say, Hideyoshi was extremely grateful, commending both Yoshimasa and Yoshikatsu the following year.

Descending the mountain, I picked my way over the huge roots and tiny bridges that crossed the "moats," and once again continued on down the wooded slope of the old Nakasendo. In a short while, I passed an old dilapidated teahouse, in use until a decade or so ago—the Yamamura Chaya—and a number of unoccupied old wooden houses. Coming up to a bend in the road, I could hear the sound of voices and, turning the corner, arrived at the Koi Iwa (鯉岩), or "Carp Boulder," so known because of its former appearance. This huge boulder, perhaps thirty feet high, once resembled a carp swimming upstream, but during the great Nobi earthquake of 1892, it turned on its side and its former resemblance was all but lost. A local story has it as follows.

> During the Kamakura period, there was a general who was ordered to go off to war. Although he was resigned to his duty as a warrior, there was one thing that weighed on his mind: he would have to leave his lover [恋人, koibito]. The two of them went and stood before Koi Iwa and made this pledge: "No matter how long we are separated, our love will be as unmovable as this boulder." The

general then promised, "If I return alive, we will meet right here." Saying this, he went off to the battle.

When his lover heard that the battle was over, she waited at the boulder every day. Finally, the general returned, the two of them met again, and were happily married. Years later, they visited the boulder once again, remembering their pledge deep in their hearts.

The boulder is now covered with vegetation and moss, and Japanese tourists were taking commemorative photos of it before walking the few yards back to Tsumago, the next post town.

COURSE TIME

Midono-shuku to Tsumago-shuku: 6 kilometers (4.2 miles). 2 hours.

13 Tsumago

そのかみを思えば夢かうつつかも夜は時雨の雨を聞きつつ

Thinking of those old days,
were they a dream or real?
At night I listen
to the steady sound
of the autumn rain.

—Ryokan

ALTHOUGH TSUMAGO was at the junction of the important road to Ina and bustling with travelers, when Okada Zenkuro passed through, he assessed it as

> much colder than Magome, with few rice or vegetable fields. The maintenance of the post town is poor, and many of the town leaders are in debt. The lower classes get by by guiding the people and horses that pass through; during the seasons of official logging, many of them work on a daily employment system.

When the Japanese railway Chuo-sen was constructed through the Kiso River valley in 1911, Tsumago even lost its role as a post town and gradually turned into a deserted village. Photos from the forties, fifties, and even the early sixties show dilapidated buildings and muddy streets and reflect the economic and psychological depression the commercial bypass had inflicted on the town. Still, the lack of real modernization turned out to be the town's salvation, for a movement to preserve historical structures after the styles of the Edo and Meiji periods was started in 1968, and in the next three years some twenty structures underwent repair and restoration. Since that time, the entire village has been brought back to nearly its original post town appearance with the removal of electricity poles and TV antennas. The old road—narrow and winding and off-limits to cars and trucks—is lined with trees and in full view of the mountains. Tsumago is now the jewel of the Kiso Road. The *Konjaku nakasendo hitori annai* describes the town in this way: "The town of Tsumago is just like a movie set. It has a row of stores and houses that brings the long ago back to the present."

It is, however, not a movie set at all, so there are no ninjas, samurai, or geishas on the streets—only people going about their jobs, Japanese visitors wanting to stay a night or two in inns where their grandparents and even more distant ancestors might have lodged, and a few foreign tourists who have fled the hypermodern big cities of Japan and gotten off the beaten track. The souvenir shops still offer many of the items they sold to travelers back in the Edo and early Meiji periods—lacquerware boxes and chopsticks, handcrafted children's toys, oiled paper umbrellas, and medicines concocted from mountain herbs—and the small, often open-air restaurants still serve the soba noodles and *gohei* mochi that beckoned pilgrims, samurai on official business, and sightseers four hundred years ago. The buildings, too, are as they were two or three hundred years ago—wooden two-story structures, with wood-slatted windows and small balconies that overhang the narrow street, the old Kiso Road.

With a last look at the *koi iwa,* I passed by the site of the Kuchi-dome bansho, a barrier established in 1602 to control movement on the Kiso, Mino, and Ina Roads. It was abandoned in 1620, its function presumed by the barrier at Kiso Fukushima, and is now nothing but a small open field surrounded by low stone walls suggesting great age. Shortly to the right is a large, old wooden notice board, announcing information for the traveler and marking the northern entrance to the town. To the left is an ancient waterwheel—there are one or two others on the walk over from Midono—and an adjoining hut, furthering the rustic feeling of the place.

In a three-minute walk I was at my inn, the Fujioto, a nice blend of the old and new. It was established in 1905 but has been modernized enough to make it quite comfortable for the Western traveler: thick, soft futons, Western-style toilets, a large wooden bath open from noon, and a dining hall where guests are seated on chairs. Foreign travelers like this place for all these reasons but also because the proprietor, Yohei, who now greeted me with a big smile at the entranceway, speaks some English, Italian, French, and German. A friendly balding man in his mid-fifties, he checked my backpack and, looking sympathetically at my wet clothing, told me that the bath was almost ready. I thanked him for his kindness and told him that I would be back soon but first wanted to walk around town.

Which was not quite the truth because I now headed back up the street to the Ko Sabo, a comfortable coffee house occupying a reconstructed Edo-period structure and now provisioned with low Japanese cypress tables, *zabuton* (cushions used for sitting on the floor), displays of local traditional artwork, and koto music wafting from an upstairs room. The o-kami-san, Yasuko Matsuse, greeted me with a happy laugh—it had been two years since my wife, Emily, our eight-year-old son, Henry, and I stopped by—and, after glancing at my clothes, launched into a children's song about the rain: "Ame ame fure fure, Kaa-chan wa . . ." I joined in the chorus, and she then quickly brought me a cup of hot coffee.

Yasuko and her husband are both quite knowledgeable about the Kiso—he is on the preservation board, and it was he who restored the old building that is now the Ko Sabo. We talked a bit about the ancient culture of the area, and she expressed the opinion that modern Japanese have gone astray with their diet and manner of living. Better, she said, would be the Jomon way of houses low to the ground and a more natural cuisine. The Jomon were for the most part hunters and gatherers, and the first identifiable people in Japan, living along the Kiso and elsewhere until about 200 B.C.E., when they were pushed north by the new Yayoi agricultural culture. I suggested that the Jomon were actually precursors of the Ainu—the "native" people living mostly in the northern island of Hokkaido—but Yasuko would have none of it. I noted the interesting similarity between the elaborate pottery designs of the Jomon people and the cloth markings of the present-day Ainu, and Yasuko countered with the fact that the Ainu make no pottery today. I conceded her point and asked for another cup.

At last, the rain had stopped completely, but there were no other customers at the Ko Sabo, and Yasuko suggested that we drive back to the Tokakuji to see if the priest had returned. We locked up the coffee shop, in a few minutes Yasuko drove up in a new Toyota, and off we went up the winding roads back to Midono. I was once again surprised—and just maybe a little alarmed—at the speed people drive on these narrow one-way streets but tried to look calm even when we suddenly encountered a car coming straight for us from the other direction. Both drivers stopped in time; the driver of the other car backed up into one of the many turnarounds and allowed us to pass. A side-glance at Yasuko revealed the same happy expression she has when serving coffee, so I guessed this was common fare.

After a few more hair-raising turns, we passed through the town of Midono and pulled up in front of the Tokakuji. At the entrance to the priest's quarters, Yasuko rang the bell, but still no one was at home. She is a good friend of both the priest and his wife, and I had been hoping for a little extra tour, but not this time. We turned back to the glass-encased shrine with the Enku figures, and I noticed for the first time that behind them were statues of Emma-O and the "Ten Kings of Hell." These are the deities that pass judgment on a soul when it has descended into the nether regions after death and are almost always depicted with scary open-mouthed faces and holding something like a pitchfork or sword. Emma-O, the ruler of hell, sits behind a table with documents in which are recorded all your sins. You've had it; there's no escape. Still, very often there will be Jizo—the bodhisattva of compassion—peeking out from farther back, letting you know that it's all an illusion, and all you have to do is wake up. In the case behind the kings here at the Tokakuji, however, there is no Jizo, but Amida Buddha, who more or less delivers the same message: give up your idea of self, and there will be no one to be in hell.

After bows and coins in the offering box, we got back in the car and headed for home, stopping at the stone monument inscribed with a poem written by the poet/monk Ryokan (1758–1831) as he passed through. The monument is located fifteen or twenty feet from the road up a wet, weed-choked path, but we stumbled up the incline to take a look. The dark stone—about three and half feet high—was soaked with rain, and the calligraphy was difficult to make out, but we were finally able to decipher it, and I wrote it down on my notepad.

この暮れのもの悲しさに若草の妻呼びたててこ牡鹿鳴くも

> In the loneliness
> of this evening
> the young male deer
> calls for his mate
> among green leaves.

Ryokan was known for his poetry in Chinese and Japanese, his simple living, and his whole-hearted participation in games with village children. He seems to have been lonely but happy, having an involvement with only one woman in his life, and that at the age of sixty-eight. It is easy to imagine him wandering through the Kiso in his tattered robe, begging as he went, enjoying the natural beauty of the place, and no doubt sleeping in the poorest of inns.

As for myself, I was happy to be staying the night at my comfortable inn with its gracious host, view of distant mist-covered mountains from my window, and the promise of an excellent dinner. Ryokan would likely have had none of these but would have been pleased with whatever his accommodations might have been.

In a few minutes' drive, we arrived back at the Ko Sabo. I thanked Yasuko for all her trouble and headed down the street to the Fujioto, where Yohei greeted me once again and showed me up the old wooden steps to my room on the second floor. Tea and rice cakes had been placed on the low table, and I was ready for a short rest.

The bath at the Fujioto is much like the one at the Yakiyama no Yu, but without a view. Floor, walls, and tub are all made of wood—probably cedar—and an antechamber for disrobing was separated from the bath by sliding frosted glass doors. The tub is a small one—just big enough for two people—so there is a lock on the door to guarantee privacy. After putting my clothes in the wooden cubby, I entered the bathing room, washed myself completely down, and rinsed. Then I slowly slid into the hot water and let go of everything—blisters, steep inclines, rain, overstuffed backpack, and editors back home who would want to know how I was spending my time. Well, this was it: quietly singing Japanese children's songs to myself as I soaked into semiconsciousness. What better way?

Back in my room, I leaned back, opened my pretty copy of the *Analects* to see if Confucius said anything about relaxing in a bath. Nothing about a bath, but there was this:

子之燕居、申申如也、夭夭如也

When the Master relaxed, he was at ease and with a radiant smile.

The *Analects*, a record of the words and deeds of Confucius, has set the standards of behavior for people in the Far East for at least two thousand years, and with this phrase I felt that even sinking into a pleasant bath, I was on the path of the Master. Checking my Chinese-Japanese dictionary for the meaning of "relax" 燕, I found that it originally was to suggest the flight of a swallow, the perfect image of easy and graceful flight.

Yohei soon called me down to the dining room for dinner, which consisted of several kinds of river fish, eggplant covered with a thick miso sauce, two small plates of mountain vegetables, rice, miso soup, and Japanese tea. I asked for and was served a small container of hot sake and dined quietly by myself. Two other tables were seated with foreigners—Germans and French, I thought—and the rest were Japanese tourists, who, by their looks, were quite pleased with their accommodations.

It was dark outside by the time I finished my sake, and although the others guests all seemed to be returning to their rooms, the rain had completely cleared up, and I decided to take a walk through the post town before bed. The road through Tsumago is narrow—more so than in the other towns—and the tiny overhanging balconies, big enough for a potted plant or two on the second floor of the old wooden buildings, shut out most of the night sky. Still, there are almost no street lamps, and the light coming from the inns lining the street all comes muted through sliding paper-and-wood doors and windows. As I looked up through the dark, I saw that the thin strip of sky was full of stars. The haiku poet Issa could have been standing in the same spot when he wrote,

> 木曽山に流れ入り天の川
> Flowing right in
> to the Kiso Mountains:
> the Milky Way.

Although the streets are busy during daylight hours, the shops close a little after sunset, and no one was about. The evening meals had been finished at most of the inns, the guests had gone to bed early, and there was just enough light for following the winding road through the town. At the southern outskirt, there was one small shop that was still open, a bar with only four or five stools where the few customers could sit and have the last beer or sake of the night. There is no other such shop in Tsumago, the local council having declared that such establishments would not add to the flavor of the post town. Nevertheless, Yohei had explained to me previously that the operator of this shop, a Ms. Aoki, was a single woman with two children whose husband had been killed by a bear some years ago. The family was an old one in Tsumago, and no one was willing to see the woman moving elsewhere to an unknown fate, so an exception was made, and she was able to eke out a living there on the edge of town. Red lanterns were hung on either side of the sliding opaque glass doors, and the tiny slatted wooden building seemed so old that it might fall down at any moment. Two two-foot-tall stone statues of local gods stood on either side of the entranceway, perhaps guarding the family from any further misfortune. Quiet voices were coming from inside, and I turned back to my inn, just beginning to shiver from the cold. I was ready to get to my futon and, after a quick fifteen-minute walk under the river of stars, descended the stone steps to the Fujioto, wished my host—who was still there at the front desk—good night, and turned in.

AFTER A FINE JAPANESE BREAKFAST, I went back upstairs, straightened up my room, and headed out onto the street. Yohei had been thoughtful enough to stuff my rain-soaked boots with newspaper the night before, and they were now passably dry. And after a good night's sleep, I was ready to walk the town.

A large part of the northern end of the post town had suffered from fires at different periods, but the rebuilding and preservation efforts were accomplished with care and attention to detail, and as I walked south, it was difficult to notice any change in authenticity.

After I passed the line of old shops, private houses, and inns, the old waki-honjin on my right was the first place of note, behind the stone gate of which was included the commission agency and the residence of the village headman. Reconstructed in 1877, the building had once included a sake brewery and thus had a number of material assets that added to its prosperity. The three-story structure now includes a samurai entrance and garden, and, as a surprise attraction, there is a small two-tatami bathroom—read, toilet—especially made by two carpenters called in from Kyoto, for the exclusive use of Emperor Meiji when he passed through on his tour of the Kiso.

The interior of the waki-honjin is spacious, with a central hearth, which is kept filled with burning embers, all the rafters dark with the smoke of generations. After sitting on the tatami floor with some Japanese tourists and listening to the explanations of our guide, we all walked around the building, admired the garden that ran parallel to a long veranda, viewed the emperor's toilet, and finally followed the signs to the attached museum. This is worth the meager entrance fee even for the non-Japanese-reading visitor. There are a number of displays of the old tools and implements used by the foresters during the Edo and Meiji periods and some cautionary scrolls depicting the fate of those unfortunates who were desperate enough to try to take lumber or even just branches of the trees for themselves. The customary rule of "one branch, one head" was illustrated clearly enough. The Owari lords were quite serious about preserving the forests for their own needs and were not hesitant to make examples of offenders. Other happier exhibits included the pottery and material remains of the Jomon people who had once lived in the area and, at the very end, behind shatterproof glass, a number of small statues by Enku.

Back out on the street, I wondered again about the people who had passed along this road for the last two millennia: the Jomon hunters and gatherers who made such intricately designed pottery; Yoshinaka's troops as they marched to Kyoto; the poets Saigyo, Basho, Ryokan, and Santoka; the swordsman Miyamoto Musashi; all the feudal lords and their serious samurai; the merchants and happy pilgrims; people escaping from village drudgery just out to have a good time; the emperor Meiji—and all on such a narrow road. In the company of so many from the past, one rarely feels alone.

Continuing to walk in toward the central part of town, on the right I passed the miniscule post office that has been in operation since Meiji times (ATM available), and then, on the left side of the street, I dropped in at the tiny tourist office where the traveler can purchase postcards with pictures of nineteenth-century woodblock prints of the Kiso, a walking stick, and *kumayoke*—the small brass bells to warn bears of your presence. This last item is "rented" to walkers but with a two-thousand-yen deposit to be returned upon arrival at the next town. To my knowledge, no one, including myself, ever returns these little bells but keeps them as souvenirs of their safe trek across the Magome Toge, the last pass if walking in a southerly direction. This is implicit at the tourist office—an old wooden structure up some rough-hewn stone steps—and the people working there are sure to point out that each bell has a different timbre, encouraging you to try a few before choosing your "rental."

I purchased some postcards and chose a bell—the lady in the office behind the window making sure that I got the right one—and then navigated back down the stone steps to the street and passed through the old *masugata,* a square-shaped village center common to most of the post towns on the Kiso, built to slow down any enemy invasion. Here, the road splits in two—an *ishitatami* path to the right, which is the old Kiso Road, and a continuance of the narrow paved road to the left.

A few more paces, and once again on the left there is an old stone wall that marks the site of a former stronghold that existed sometime in the mid-1500s. I climbed the stone steps along this wall, passed a five-hundred-year-old cherry tree growing from a level part of the old fortress, and arrived at the Kotokuji, a Rinzai Zen temple said to have been founded in 1500, but at that time in a different location. Entering the main gate on the left, one finds a sandy open ground facing the main hall, established in 1725. The floorboard is of the *uguisubari* type, constructed of boards that sound like a nightingale when walked on, so to make the priests aware of intruders at night. Such devices were usually used in the residences of daimyo, their advisors, and aristocrats, and one wonders why they might be needed in a Buddhist temple. Over the temple doors is a huge wooden placard engraved with the characters 光徳寺殿—*kotokujiden*—brushed by the swordsman/artist Yamaoka Tesshu. Hanging just inside the entrance to the priests' quarters on the right is a unique palanquin—one with wheels—supposedly invented by the man who was abbot there between 1830 and 1844. As I chatted with the head priest, he told me that the abbot loved this palanquin so much that he had once ridden it all the way to Kyoto. I expressed the hope that the good abbot had had a lot of cushions, and he laughed and agreed that it must have been a very bumpy ride.

Outside of the temple gate, I noticed a small monument—a place to pray and make offerings for the souls of deceased "beasts, birds, and fish." This is not exactly a dog or cat cemetery, but I'm unaware of there being such a place dedicated to small animals at any church or temple back home. I stopped for a moment, put my palms together for all the dogs and cats I have been blessed with in my life, left a hundred yen in the offering box, and went carefully back down the steep stone steps.

At the bottom of the steps is a small temple dedicated to Jizo (the Buddhist protective saint of children, travelers, and small animals) and next to it a large stone engraving of Kanzan and Jittoku, two eccentric Chinese Buddhist monks from the T'ang period who confounded people with their antics and poetry. Interestingly, the sign next to this stone explains that this large stone was found after an earthquake in 1984 and was thought to be an engraving of *dosojin*. Why it was in the Tsumago area, who carved it, and when are unknown.

Taking the *ishitatami*-laid old Nakasendo path to the right, I passed the Matsushiro-ya, one of the oldest inns on the Kiso Road. The two-story structure is of slatted wood, and the wide entranceway is almost always open; what would be the wall to the left consists of two large sliding paper doors, which are also almost always open. This provides the traveler a look inside and gives the place an airy, open atmosphere, and facing the entranceway is a bank of large red-orange azalea bushes. The interior of the inn is also all wood with tatami floors; there are no telephones or television sets, and the only modern convenience is a pair of Western toilets. The old signboards inviting travelers to stop can still be seen on the upper story over the entrance to the inn. When I stayed there with my wife and some friends once years ago, I asked the proprietor what generation master he was, and he replied, "Well, I'm the nineteenth generation in this building, but the inn burned down and was then rebuilt in the Edo period, and all the old records were lost. So we really don't know how many generations we go back before that."

I tried to recall how many of the generations of my own family line I could identify: six at the most. I thought of Mrs. Hotta and the mortuary tablets of the generations of her ancestors in Agematsu, and of Mineko's husband's ancestral graves in Kiso Fukushima, and wondered how different their sense of place must be than that of my own.

Beyond the Matsudaira-ya the line of shops and inns continues for perhaps an eighth of a mile. One or two of the cheaper inns for travelers and their horses have been preserved but are only showcases now. Accommodations were simply raised wooden platforms next to the stalls, and looking in, a haiku by Basho came immediately to mind.

蚤虱馬の尿する枕もと

Fleas and lice,
the horse pissing
next to my pillow.

It was now late in the afternoon, but I continued to walk past the old shops, each with double-wide open entrances, so the traveler can get a better look at their wares. Here is a place offering boxes and chopsticks made of cedar wood; there, a tiny store with kimonos and yukata made of antique cotton and silk; and another with displays of traditional toys all made locally from local wood and paper. There is also a fine sake shop with rows of the very best— my favorites being Masumi, "True Clarity," from a brewery established in 1662 and Nanawarai, "Seven Laughs," which has been making people happy since 1892. Finally, at the edge of town, Ms. Aoki's *izakaya* was still closed and quiet, and I turned back toward the Fujioto, another long bath, and a rest before dinner.

At six o'clock, Ichikawa-san, his daughter Seiko, who speaks perfect English although she has never been to the States or Great Britain, and his sometime English teacher, Motoko, arrived at the inn for a ten-course dinner. I met my friend Ichikawa-san in 1967 when I taught my first English classes at the Nagoya YMCA— something like a country club in Japan—and thought from his youthful expression that he must have been a rather erudite sixteen-year-old. It turned out that he was thirty-four and a teacher of Japanese literature at night school. His weekends were reserved for mountain climbing, an avocation he continued through his seventies. Now in his eighties and in declining health, he practices yoga, continues to study English, and, as he did back in Kiso Fukushima, is always ready to help out his old friend whenever he can. We ate, laughed, and talked, mostly about the mountains we had climbed together—Ontake, Komagatake, Fuji (where I had been scared half to death by a passing lightning storm), and Hakusan, where, had Ichikawa-san not taught me the proper use of an ice pick as a restraining device, I would probably still be buried under thirty feet of snow and ice. And, of course, we shared cup after cup of sake. Finally, the evening drew to a close, Ichikawa-san sneaked out to pay the entire bill, and he, his daughter, and friend drove off into the night. Humble and generous to a fault, he has taught me more about Japanese culture and literature than I have learned from all the books I've ever read, and, as I watched the red taillights of his car disappear around the bend, I wondered if this would be his final friendly gesture and goodbye. Living alone in his tiny hut deep in the forests around Mount Ena, he was as at ease as Confucius's swallow in the mountains he loves so much. I waved, yelled, "Sayonara," and headed upstairs to bed.

I WAS UP EARLY, with no sake headache from the night before, the forecast was for a sunny day, and the clouds beneath the western mountains across the valley were a bright white from the just rising sun. The Kiso River turns away to the west at Midono, but there is a small tributary, the Hosono River, that flows by on the west side of Tsumago. I was still in a country of mountains and rivers.

Just outside of my window, there were some cherry trees filled with Japanese house sparrows and a few small buildings of weathered wood, with white clay and tile roofs. Directly across from me was a *kura*, the traditional whitewashed clay private warehouse, also with a tiled roof, and above the mist in the valley was the steep Shiroyama, where the small castle had once stood. I was once again impressed that any "moats" must have been empty ditches as it would have been extremely difficult to channel water up there.

At seven thirty, I went downstairs to a breakfast of orange juice, a banana, milk, toast, yogurt, marmalade, an egg and ham cooked over a *karo,* and coffee. I was talking with Yohei when a young woman came up and asked if she could have the same fare, but the master apologized and explained that such Western breakfasts were prepared for the night before only for guests who spent more than one night at the inn. She was clearly annoyed, but since I had one slice of bread left, I offered it to her, it went into the toaster, and everyone was pleased. Later, she pronounced, "I'm French, you see, so I can't get used to these Japanese breakfasts," and I was left to assume that we Americans must have a reputation for far less than discerning palates.

Back up in my room, I rearranged my belongings and got ready for the last walk of the trip. I would check my pack with the people at the tourist office, and they would have it transferred to their office in Magome, a nice convenience that assures an easier hike over the Magome Toge—not as steep as the Torii Toge, but longer and including a number of ascents and descents. There was only one problem: I had now obtained a hardbound copy book of the *Konjaku nakasendo hitori annai,* an invaluable source of information about the Kiso Road, complete with geographical descriptions, poetry related to the road, local tales, and just about everything I had been looking for. Now I was loath to let it out of my sight even for a moment, but I could hardly carry it in my hand over the pass. Back downstairs, I spoke to Yohei about my conundrum, and without hesitation he whisked me off to a shop that specialized in traditional cotton shoulder bags, the perfect solution. It was still too early for the shop to be open, but Yohei knocked on the glass entranceway, and the proprietress came out all smiles when she saw his face. A transaction was quickly made; we bid the woman good-bye and headed back to the Fujioto.

It was time to go. As I prepared to settle the account for my stay, Yohei explained with a smile that Ichikawa-san had not only paid for last night's dinner but also for my entire fare at the inn. I was left speechless, but Yohei, his wife, daughter, and the rest of the staff were lined up bowing me off, so with many a thank-you all around, I turned and walked the stone-paved incline up to the old Kiso Road.

When I checked my backpack at the tourist office, I was given another dose of Japanese generosity. While doing research for this trip back in Miami, I had run across a reference to the *Kisoji meisho zue*, the master guidebook to the Kiso Road written in 1805. Somehow, I was able to find a copy on Japanese Amazon and, although it was rather pricey, quickly placed an order. In less than a week, a boxed hardbound edition arrived at my doorstep, and in great anticipation, I unwrapped and then opened the book. It was a reprint of the original but written entirely in grass-script calligraphy, which would be unintelligible for most modern Japanese, not to speak of myself. With a sigh, I placed it up on the bookshelf and went back to other sources.

As I handed over my backpack and signed the paper forms, I recounted this sad tale to the man behind the office window, a Mr. Fujiwara Yoshinori. He listened with a sympathetic expression, disappeared back into the office for a moment, and then returned with a book in hand. "You mean this?" he asked and opened it to reveal the same book but entirely in modern Japanese print. I was floored and inquired how and where I might purchase a copy. "Here, take this one," he said and placed it into my hand. I tried to fight off this remarkable gesture (yes, only halfheartedly) but knew that it would be a futile effort. We talked a while longer about the Kiso Road—he had walked it in its entirety a number of times. I stuffed this second volume into my new handy shoulder satchel, walked down the stone steps, and with a deep bow, headed south.

Tsumago has its own distinct charm in the early morning, and photographers are often out just before sunrise to catch just the right shot. Mountains line either side of the village and then seem to bring it to an abrupt stop where the road turns. Tea bushes and azaleas grow alongside the road here and there, a brightly colored maple obscures a white-stucco *kura*, and the slatted wooden balconies are still dark with the early-morning dew. In a few moments, the mountains to the west will grow brighter with the rising sun, still hidden by those on the opposite side of the road. A few shop owners will be beginning to open their wide sliding glass doors on the possibility of an early customer, but most tourists are still in their inns either finishing a late breakfast or packing up their belongings up in their rooms.

This morning, no one else was on the road, the air was cold and crisp, and most of the clouds had gone to wherever it is they go on a day like this. I passed through the village with only the sound of my walking stick on the pavement and the little kumayoke bell tied to my shoulder satchel. Shortly after the Aoki izakaya at the edge of town, the road narrowed and passed through an ancient graveyard; the river appeared on my right, and again there was the sound of water. The sun was now coming up, and steam was rising off the already-harvested, cramped rice fields. Presently, the road went up an incline and then down a decline, but mostly, it seemed to me, the former. Without my pack though, I kept up a pretty good pace and quickly caught up with two young Chinese women out for a short hike. They were foreign-language students from Shanghai studying in Nagoya, they explained, and had wanted to spend a weekend in the Japanese countryside. The two of them looked at my little bell, declared it to be *kawaii* ("cute"), and asked why a grown man would wear such a thing. I did my best to explain what it was for without sounding alarming, and they giggled a little but then decided that they'd walked far enough and would turn back to Tsumago. We waved each other good-bye, and I carried on.

I now crossed the Otsuma Bridge and, as the road went steadily uphill, turned into a short length of ishitatami and ascended through a dark forest of cedar and cypress trees. There was a large kumayoke bell attached to a wooden post at the side of the path, which I rang vigorously. Farther up the steep path was a stone monument engraved with some Buddhist deity, blessing the oxen that had had to plod up and down this route with heavy loads. It was hard for me to imagine any four-legged animal navigating this path—although I knew that the warlords and others passed through on horses—and I wondered again what it must have been like for the abbot bouncing along in his wheeled palanquin. I was happy to be on foot.

Soon I passed through the old neighborhood of O-tsumago where there were koshin monuments that looked like ancient tombs and a number of very old inns. A large white dog was tied up at the entrance of one of these, but it paid no attention to me, as hikers were not exactly rarities on this stretch of the road.

In another one hundred yards, the slope became even steeper and then descended into the small hamlet of Kudaritani. In another few yards, there was another monument and the small dilapidated Kurashina Shrine. According to the *Konjaku nakasendo hitori annai*, the story connected with this shrine goes as follows:

> In July of 1585, when Toyotomi Hideyoshi was commanded to take the office of *kampaku*, the master of Matsumoto Castle, Ogasawara Jokei, sent gifts of gold, silver roosters, silkworms, cocoons, and swords with his vassal Kurashina Shichirozaemon. However, thieves who had found out about [the transport of] these treasures, killed Shichirozaemon and stole the gifts. Later, his wife visited the area, planted chestnuts there, and said, "May my husband's enemies be cursed with his spite to the number of these chestnuts." After that, there was a landslide there that swept away a village in the valley below. The villagers feared that this was due to the curse of Shichirozaemon, and thus built a small temple to enshrine his spirit.

A little farther on, a narrow path branched off to the left through the woods that led to the *otoko taki* and the *onna taki*, or the "Male and Female Falls." These are the waterfalls made famous in Yoshikawa Eiji's novel *Musashi* and are supposedly the falls under which

Musashi and Otsu, the fictional woman who relentlessly and amo-
rously pursued the famous swordsman, sat in meditation. The
Male Falls, as one might suspect, are larger and with a generous
flow of water, while the Female Falls are delicate and more of a
cascading spray. According to the old guidebooks, the pools at
the bottom of the falls were buried by earthquakes during the Edo
period, but it is a refreshing and quiet place to stop and rest. The
climb over the pass was not going to get any easier soon.

On my feet again, I climbed up some wood plank reinforced
steps, and the path came out to a narrow highway and a now-
abandoned *chaya,* where fifteen years ago my wife and I had eaten
gohei mochi and drunk green tea. I walked to my left up the highway, crossed a narrow wooden bridge, and was on the old Kiso
Road again. The cedar-lined path was now rocks and tree roots,
now sand, now short wooden bridges, or now ishitatami. How
did early travelers do this in straw sandals? The warlords must
have chosen their men for this trip very carefully.

At last, toward the top of the pass, stands the *ichikokutochi chaya,*
a wooden building over two hundred fifty years old, dark and
smoky, entirely open at the front. There are large tables at which
to sit, and an old man passes out free tea and candy (donations
are not prohibited) and will wood burn the name of the *chaya* on
walking sticks if travelers so desire. The chaya had been moved
here from lower in the valley between 1748 and 1751 and repaired
with unfinished wood. Where there was once a small barrier, there
is now a large spreading cherry tree and, beneath that, a shrine to
the Kannon of Easy Childbirth.

I sat down at one of the old wooden tables, received some tea,
and asked the old man to wood burn my walking stick. Seated
across from me was a young German couple walking toward Tsumago and then returning by bus. They were enjoying this short
hike and asked about the Kiso as it headed toward Narai. They
would try the entire road next year, they said.

Leaving a few hundred yen in the donation jar, I said good-bye to the German couple and carried on up the old road—really just a dirt path at this point. The old man had reminded me that the imperial princess Kazunomiya had made an unprecedented journey from Kyoto and stopped here in 1861 on her way to marry the fourteenth Tokugawa shogun, Iemochi. There is a story that she was secretly assassinated on the way and replaced with a commoner woman—Iemochi had never seen her—to prevent the union of the shogunate and imperial families and thus hasten the shogun's downfall, which came only few years later. Six years after Kazunomiya's procession, the "Ee ja nai ka" craze that had sprung up in Nagoya spread through the southern Kiso. The adherents of this movement danced wildly along the road to the accompaniment of flutes and drums, chanting "Ee ja nai ka, ee ja nai ka" ("Ain't it great? Ain't it great?"), dropping off their amulets here and there for the good fortune (and wonderment) of the locals.

But instead of enthusiastic dancers and singers, as I climbed steadily up the hill, I was met with some three hundred fifty high school students and their harassed-looking teacher chaperones out on a field trip. I answered cheerfully to their "Harro!" a couple of hundred times, but they soon disappeared down the old path, and, at last, I arrived at the top of Magome Toge, an elevation of 2,628 feet. At the side of the path is a teahouse, and there is a wooden road marker engraved with Masaoka Shiki's haiku:

白雲や青葉若葉の三十里
White clouds,
green leaves, young leaves,
for miles and miles.

From here, it was all downhill, and from the sand-filled courtyard of the large Kumano Shrine, I looked out to see the Nobi Plain. The end of the mountains! I continued to walk down the hill, past a neighborhood of farmhouses that had escaped all the fires since 1753. Beans and other vegetables were being dried on front porches, and long strings of persimmons were hanging from Edo-period wooden balconies. Just beyond the houses is a small graveyard with some stone monuments engraved in a Chinese script that no one but scholars can understand anymore. About three hundred yards farther down the path is a rest area and a barely legible stone monument engraved with a quote from Ikku Jippensha, the Edo-period writer whose accounts covered both the Tokaido and Nakasendo. A Japanese couple and I peered at the monument and finally were able to read the difficult script:

> I don't see any good-looking women here,
> but their chestnut rice is famous!

Continuing down the hill, there is still more ishitatami, and the path is lined with persimmon trees. At this time of year, they were bare of leaves but loaded with bright orange fruit, one of which fell and barely missed my head as I passed underneath. Down a little farther, and there was a weathered *dosojin* monument, and I made a small offering in thanks for being able to finish this walk. Finally, the path opened up to a place for viewing Mount Ena, a sacred mountain where the umbilical cord of the sun goddess Amaterasu is said to be buried and in the foothills of which lives my friend Ichikawa-san. It was a beautiful, clear day, quite a contrast to the first day of slogging through the rain up the steep road to Niekawa. Unwilling to take even a short rest, I continued down the hill to Magome, the southernmost post town on the Kiso Road.

COURSE TIME
Tsumago to Magome: 8 kilometers (4.8 miles). 2 hours, 50 minutes.

14 Magome ELEVATION I,254 FEET

大寺にひとり宿かる夜寒かな

Lodging alone
in a large temple:
how cold the night!

—Shiki

Walking down the steep, stone-paved, shop-lined street, I ducked into my favorite Magome coffee shop with its beautiful open view of Mount Ena and thought . . . nothing. This was the last of the eleven post towns, the end of the line. Huge Japanese crows were cawing somewhere in the distance, the air was clear, and from where I sat, I could see the tiled roof of a large Buddhist temple peeking through the tops of the trees far across the valley. It was the world in Emptiness—or in my case, the world in an empty mind.

I finished my lunch of an egg sandwich and banana milkshake, the shop's specialty, and continued down the steep slope. Tourists were everywhere—this was the biggest weekend for autumn colors—some of them in a pretty strange array. On one student's sweatshirt was printed, "BABY DOLL: More Joyful"; on a young lady's T-shirt, "What Lies Ahead? A journey of misery." Another T-shirt advised me to "Drink Jelly." Where did they get these, and why could I never find them when I looked for them?

Magome is the easiest town to access from the Chuo-sen national railroad in nearby Nakatsugawa, and perhaps the most prosperous of them all. Much of it was burned down in a disastrous fire in 1895, but the rebuilding was done according to traditional architecture, and on a quiet day, it still has the flavor of the old Kiso Road. In his novel *Yoakemae*, Shimazaki Toson described the town in this way.

> [Within the post town] both sides of the highway have been built up with stone walls, step by step, grade by grade, and the people's homes are constructed atop of these. To stave off the wind and snow as much as possible, rocks are placed on the wooden plank roofs of the houses, which are lined up to the right and left. . . . Although it can be said that [the town lies] in the midst of the mountains, a broad sky opens up in the direction of the foothills of Mount Ena, and the location is such that one can view the broad plain of Mino. Somehow the atmosphere of the West [Western Japan] seems to pass through the place.

Today, as I entered the post town from the north, it was exactly as described by Toson in the above passage—gradually elevated stone walls and foundations with level places on top of them upon which the houses are built. Here and there were carp ponds in front of the houses, the water collected from the subterranean gullies beneath.

But Magome was not always as lively and clean and bustling as it is today. According to the *Kiso kaido yadotsuke,* it was a "miserable post town," and the *Jinjutsu kiko* notes,

> The post town is provincial and loutish. Places that hire maidservants, serving as prostitutes, put up signs advertising "meals." There are also write-ups for money changers and the like.

When Okada Zenkuro passed through, his impression was not much better.

Although this post town is within the Kiso Valley, it is situated at the entrance to the province of Mino, and is a warm region. Thus, the rice and vegetable fields yield excellent crops, and they can grow such trees as mulberry and paper mulberry. Nevertheless, the fields are less than can support the population [only 695 people in Zenkuro's time], men and horses are employed with promises to pay later, the leaders of the post town are often in debt, and the town is in bad shape. This extends to the poorer people who, because their fields are few, keep oxen and transport goods from Fukushima and Matsumoto to Nagoya and Mino, and so make their way through the world. On the other hand, they may do such things as to become porters for travelers on pilgrimages to the Zenkoji Temple [in Nagano]. Every summer, there are those who make their living by looking after silkworms.

Descending the slope, I passed the site of the old waki-honjin, at the rear of which is a museum housing documents, implements used during the heyday of the Edo period, and real samples of the "five trees" of the Kiso. Again, in the *Yoakemae:*

> *Hinoki* 檜, *sawara* 椹, *asuhi* 明檜, *koyamaki* 高野槇 and *nezuko* 瘤—
> these were said to be the Five Trees of the Kiso. The forests where
> these trees flourished were particularly deep in the mountains . . .
> and the Owari fief, which managed the Kiso Mountians, regarded
> the excellent lumber growing in this area quite highly. Regulation
> was rigid. . . . And thus, not a single cypress was taken lightly. In
> the eyes of the officials, a single tree was more valued than the life
> of a human being.

Finally, I picked up my backpack at the tourist center, thanked the agent for making my last big hike fifty pounds lighter, took a right at a narrow alleyway, and in five minutes was slowly climbing up the long, stone, Jizo-lined stepway to the Eishoji. Although only a short distance from the main street of Magome, the surroundings are extremely quiet—even hushed. No crowds, no shop owners standing expectantly at their doorways, and no funny T-shirts: instead, I was greeted by a large statue of Kannon backed by a full red-leafed maple tree just in front of the main gate to the temple. Inside the temple grounds, I waited for the priest and his wife to arrive, which they did shortly, accompanied by a small white Pomeranian–toy poodle mix that happily ran around the gravel courtyard and then jumped into the arms of the priest's wife.

After a friendly exchange—I had stayed at this temple one night a few years ago—I was shown to my sleeping quarters, a *shukubo,* or lodging for students and travelers. This consisted of two tatami-floored rooms accoutered with a low table and some cushions for sitting. The futon were packed away inside the closets, and in the *tokonoma,* or alcove, was a simple arrangement of some purple bellflowers in an unglazed pot and a scroll brushed with the character 忍, "patience." The toilets were back down a narrow wooden walkway, and the bath back near the entrance of the temple proper.

Tired from the walk, I took the small pillow out of the closet and got ready to recline in the silence of the temple. Barely visible through the open sliding paper doors was the elaborate temple garden—more maples, azaleas, and a few pines on the bordering hill, a number of large rocks placed artfully throughout the thousand-square-foot area, and a shallow pond with water lilies suggesting a marsh. Carp spotted with orange, white, and black swam lazily back and forth. The sky was still relatively cloudless. I could feel sleep mercifully creeping up on me. I closed my eyes, and . . .

"Hello! Wilson-san!" Sitting bolt upright, I saw that it was my friend and benefactor, Mr. Hida, a former middle-school principal, an expert on the Kiso Road, and a particular fan of the poetry of Santoka. He was also a good friend of the resident priest and had arranged my stay overnight here, now for the second time. After a happy handshake, tea and bean cakes, and a short conversation, he announced that he had business in Magome but would meet me here for dinner tonight. With a television cameraman. For an interview. What? Well, OK. I got up and saw him off at the edge of the garden, went back to my room, and slipped into dreams of walking—walking, past stone carvings of all the Buddhist and local gods that had protected me along the way, and tiny tingling bells.

The Eishoji is a large Rinzai Zen temple high up on a hill. Founded in 1661, the main temple was built between 1789 and 1801. In the Kannon Hall at the side of the main temple is enshrined a wooden statue of Amida Nyorai about eighteen feet tall, carved from a single piece of cypress during the latter part of the Heian period. The temple is the *bodaiji,* not just for the Shimazaki family, but for many others who have lived in Magome for hundreds of years, and in a large room in the back of the main hall are all of the memorial tablets that mark generations of ancestors. In the middle of a rice field just west of the temple complex is a place called the Bikunidera, "Nun's Temple," where stand eight stone pagodas. They had been placed there in some confusion, and some of them lacked the traditional five stones representing the elements of wind, emptiness, fire, water, and earth. Thus, the temple may have originally been connected with the esoteric Buddhist sects of Shingon or Tendai, but records of this are no longer extant.

After an hour or so, the priest's wife visited my room to announce that the bath was ready. She was holding her little dog, which had been destined to be "discarded" because it was not quite show material. She and her husband—both in their fifties—adopted the little thing just before it was to be put down: Buddhist compassion and people after my own heart.

After a twenty-minute soak in a tiny, but comfortable wooden bath, I made my way to the room where we would be served dinner. Hida-san and I sat on cushions at a low table, and the priest set out red and black lacquerware trays and bowls of *shojin ryori,* a formal vegetarian meal for Buddhist priests. Tonight we would have grilled eggplant, three different kinds of potatoes, cooked soy beans (marinated in sugar, soy sauce, and, no doubt, a number of other ingredients), ginger, two different preparations of tofu, miso soup, and beer. And sure enough, a cameraman from a local Nagoya TV station had shown up to interview me. Hidasan, a big man with a constant smile, was happy and effusive, and in between the cameraman's questions of "What are your impressions of the meal? Magome? The Kiso Road?" we laughed and talked about Santoka and what it meant to walk solo along this road, which Hida-san had done many times. He has obviously retained the mode of a teacher all these years and enthusiastically lectured the cameraman as the Zen priest explained the very elegant and delicious meal.

After dinner, the priest's wife, white dog still in her lap, drove us to a bar outside of town that Hida-san had patronized since his college days and then during his long term as a middle-school principal. This establishment is really only one large open room with tables, in front of which is a bar with about ten stools. Tonight there was only one customer, an old man who had clearly had a few, sitting at the polished wood bar, smoking, and singing into the karaoke machine; another elderly fellow peeling three box loads of persimmons to string and hang from balconies as *hoshigaki;* the seventyish smiling o-kami-san; and a fifteen-year-old cat that had once, long ago, come in out of the cold and decided to stay. Hida-san ordered Nanawarai sake, grilled mackerel pike, and then *kotsuzake.* Then, in between courses, he stepped up to the microphone and belted out remarkably melodious versions of "The Rose" in both English and Japanese. How the Japanese love to sing! It was no accident that karaoke was invented in this country.

Finally, the priest appeared at the door, knocked down a quick tumbler of sake, and drove us back in the dark rain to the temple. On the winding way home, Hida-san delivered a lecture on *kamemushi,* a kind of stink bug that proliferates in the fall and the presence of which presages heavy snows in the winter. They look like little black turtles, he explained, and hence their name, "turtle bug." *Kamemushi* eat mulberries in the summer and come into people's houses in the fall to escape the cold. They hide in the bedding where no one can see them until it's too late: touch them, and they exude a nasty smell that permeates the entire room. I saw them in my rooms in Nojiri and the Yakiyama no Yu but left them alone: Buddhist noninterference. No problem.

Arriving back at the temple, my friend gave me a deep, smiling bow, jumped into his own car, and drove the twenty or so miles back home. Hida-san, a first-rate raconteur, is descended from the Hida Genji, and his family has strong ties with the Kiso Valley.

Exhausted from all the talk and singing, I bid the priest good night and walked down the wooden corridor to my room. With a quick check for the dreaded turtle bug, I spread out my bedding and drifted off into my last night on the Kiso Road.

IN THE MORNING I woke up with the sensation that my futon was made of ice. I had awakened a few times during the night, turned on the gas heater, and then thought better of it after warming up a bit. Zen priests are supposed to be tough, and maybe the sleeping quarters are designed to help make them so. The thin walls, if not of paper themselves, are constructed of clay and straw and notoriously ill fitted against falling temperatures. This is true of most traditional Japanese houses and, along with their relatively high elevation off the ground, suggests a Polynesian element to the early populating of the Japanese islands. The language is Ural-Altaic, however, and the grammar very close to Korean. Korea is one of the coldest places I've ever been in my life and where the heating system, the *ondul,* coils underneath the houses permeating up through a sort of lacquered floor. If some of the first migrants moved through Korea on their way to the Japanese archipelago, they somehow missed this practical and warm device against the cold, and I was paying for their oversight.

Such thoughts aside, this was indeed the coldest night I had spent on the Kiso, and I wondered about Zenkuro's assessment of Magome being "in a warm region." I looked at the scroll in the alcove—忍, "patience"—and tried to take heart.

The morning, however, was bright and clear, and I had a beautiful view of pink and light green mountains outside of the open sliding paper doors. After arranging my backpack and, once again, checking to make sure that no *kamemushi* had snuggled into my clean pairs of underwear or socks, I wandered down the corridor to find that a *shojin ryori* breakfast had already been laid out for me on the low table. I was pleased to see that there was plenty of coffee— not the usual fare in a Zen temple—and after a leisurely chat with the priest and his wife, I was ready to go. At the entranceway, he generously presented me with a small copy of a poem done in Shimazaki Toson's own hand as a souvenir. It was on a hard, flat piece of cardboard-like paper, brushed in an indecipherable grass script, and just about the only thing I could have squeezed into my pack.

After tying on my boots at the front wooden steps, I walked out to the white gravel courtyard, accompanied part way by the frisky little white dog, bowed several times to the priest and his wife, and descended the stone stairway that would lead me back to Magome. It was still too early for tourists and so was a quiet walk down to the southern end of town, past the huge old waterwheel at the square. At the bottom of the slope, and after passing the bus station and its shops, the road split into three: the one going straight to the southwest being the Nakasendo. It was remarkable how quickly the atmosphere had changed. Just as the mountains seemed to snap shut on the road at Niekawa, they had now snapped open, and I was in the middle of open fields, low hills, and an open sky. Somehow I was breathing more easily, and my pace had picked up.

In what seemed like a very short time, I passed through the hamlet of Aramachi and could see a small rise on the right of the road, the site of Magome Castle. According to the sign, Kiso Yoshimasa had put his general Shimazaki Shigemichi in charge of the castle, but in 1584 it was attacked by the forces of Tokugawa Ieyasu, and Shigemichi fled to Tsumago Castle. Later, Yoshimasa was moved to a different fief, and Shigemichi came down from Tsumago to work the fields and open up the post town of Magome.

The road now followed a winding path mostly downhill, and on the left was a *torii* gate and a dark row of cedar trees indicating the entrance to another branch of the Suwa Shrine.

In the sixth month of 1892, at the age of twenty-five, the haiku poet and journalist Masaoka Shiki fled his college exams and, instead, decided to follow the footsteps of Basho's travel diary, *Sarashina nikki.* In his own journal, *Kakehashi no ki,* he wrote,

> I woke up early, but the rain had not stopped, so I asked the maid at my inn to buy me a raincoat. Going down the hill from Magome, the rice paddies and fields opened up a bit between the mountains, and [I could see that] the ears of barley were still yellow. In the Kiso Valley, if there is one little inch of land, a mulberry tree is planted; if there is one single house standing, you are sure to be given up as food for fleas. But arriving here, it had the feeling of a different world.

桑の実木曽路出づれば穂波かな
Leaving the Kiso Road
and its mulberry nuts:
waving fields of grain.

A stone monument engraved with this haiku stands here in a small open field.

In less than a mile, I reached the western edge of Shinchaya, at the edge of which is a stone marker indicating the boundary of Mino and Shinano Provinces. I couldn't resist and did what I suppose everyone who passes through does: put one foot in the old province of Mino and the other in Shinano. A short distance away was a stone monument engraved with Basho's haiku,

送られつ送りつ果ては木曽の穐
Sending them off,
being sent off:
the Kiso in autumn.

And another large monument, placed here only in 1952 and engraved in Toson's hand, reads,

是より北木曽路
From here north, the Kiso Road

I had come to the end of the Kiso Road, if not quite the end of my walk.

About a hundred yards ahead, the Nakasendo turned away from the road and headed straight west, winding back and forth—much on ishitatami—through a beautifully wooded area. This was the Jikkyoku Pass (十曲峠), so named for its ten curves.

At last, the steep road gave out, and I passed through the hamlet of Yamanaka. In about a hundred fifty yards, the Ioji, a temple housing Yakushi Nyorai, the "Medicine Buddha," appeared on my left. Engraved on a stone monument at the entrance, I could barely make out the last of our haiku from Basho.

梅が香にのつと日の出る山路かな
The scent of plum blossoms:
suddenly the sun comes out
on this mountain road!

There is also an old placard advertising the sale of Fox Ointment (狐膏薬), apparently sold in this village long ago. In the *Zoku hizakurige,* a barker is doing his best to make a sale:

Well, well, come along and buy some, please. Why, this famed Fox Ointment right here will cure sore feet, cuts, sword wounds, boils or abscesses. No matter where they are, just one application will do the trick. And more, keeping it close at hand to use again and again is like a rich man keeping his gold and silver close by. . . . Buy some for a rainy day!

I asked a nearby shop owner if this magic medicine was still available, but he just laughed and waved me off. So I decided on the next best thing: making my way down into the old post town of Ochiai, past the former sites of the honjin and waki-honjin—now long gone—walking by the Zenshoji temple, and finding the Miyama Coffee Shop, also the final stop of my walk with Robbie and Gary.

> Ochiai has about ninety houses. West of here, there are still slopes here and there, but you are now out of the deep mountains, there are no more dangerous steep places, and your mind is at ease. Leaving the Kiso Road and coming out into this place, you feel for the first time that you have come home.
>
> —Kaibara Ekiken

After a good cup of thick Japanese coffee, I caught a cab, took a quick ride to the Chuo-sen railroad station at nearby Nakatsugawa, and started my way back to Tokyo, and then Miami.

The trip was over. The Kiso Valley would soon lose its autumn foliage, the temperature would drop precipitously, and any tracks I left would be covered by the cold winter rains and snow.

COURSE TIME
Magome to Ochiai: 4.5 kilometers (2.7 miles). 2 hours.

Afterword

PEOPLE WALK for all kinds of reasons. Socrates, Nietzsche, and Kant famously walked in order to think. Confined within four walls and physically stagnant, they felt their thought processes were stultified and restrained. Thoreau and Muir both walked to become more alive by immersing themselves in the wild. "Life consists of wildness," Thoreau wrote, "and the most alive is the wildest."

The Japanese poets Saigyo and Basho walked to gain aesthetic perspective by freeing themselves from the familiar and habitual. Santoka, another Japanese poet, said that he walked because it was the only thing he could do besides drink sake and scribble haiku. He spent almost thirty-five years on the road.

On a practical level, all of us, particularly elderly or sedentary persons, are encouraged to walk for our health, to get the blood moving through our bodies and brains. Working our thigh muscles, the largest muscles in the body, effectively pumps oxygen and nutrients through our entire systems. Of course, many people also walk as their primary mode of transportation, and others just to get out of the house.

In my own case, I have always liked long walks for the same reason that I enjoyed running track in junior and senior high school and jogging in later years. The cadence my body settles into after the first ten or fifteen minutes puts my mind in a meditative state that edges out the peripheral clutter that often lodges there. Unlike the great philosophers, I do not find walking or running a wellspring of deep thought, or really any thought at all.

Which brings me to another reason I love to walk: to participate fully in the rhythm not just of my own body, but of the environment around me. With my consciousness freed from the distraction of nagging, scattered thoughts, I can see, hear, smell, and feel my surroundings in a way that I normally don't, partaking of it all with every step. This frame of mind is often referred to as being "present" or "engaged," and when I walk, I can attain it effortlessly.

SIMILARLY, people travel for different reasons. Some travel for recreation, others to see new sights and meet new people, still others to get away from their jobs and homes, to loosen the fetters that bind them to their everyday lives. The problem with modern travel is that we often take our everyday lives with us, in every way that it is possible to do so. What kind of clothes will I need? What items can't I do without? What will I read or watch? How will I stay in touch with family and friends? Should I take my iPod, iPad, iPhone, Nook, Kindle, laptop?

The ancients in Japan and China called travel *hyohaku* (漂泊), the kanji meaning "to float along on a river or stream, following the eddies and swirls of the current" and "to tie up for the night." This is letting go and moving freely. Fitting the bare necessities into a backpack and doing without accustomed luxuries may bring its discomforts, but comfort is rarely the objective of travel. We are comfortable enough at home. If you are looking for five-star hotels, you can likely find one close to your home and save the bulk of your travel expenses.

Happily, modern travel offers many modes of conveyance, but this can also have a downside. Usually, we get to Europe or the Far East by airplane and then take a bus or taxi from the airport to our hotel. After that, side trips and visits to local attractions often require more taxi, bus, tram, or boat rides, which end up consuming a good bit of our travel time, so that our feet rarely touch the ground. In Japan they call this a "Daruma journey" (達磨旅行), after the Zen patriarch who sat for so long that his legs fell off.

If we travel seeking new experiences beyond photo opportunities and local cuisine, these days we often fall short of having them. Like Edo-period warlords, we ride along in modern-day palanquins, emerging at our destinations and missing everything in between. Arriving at a post town by train or bus, we are cheated of the satisfaction of slower but steady progress on foot, tantalizing views of our goal in the distance, the sweet anticipation of a journey's end. But when we bypass the tiny teahouse selling *gohei* mochi (soft rice cakes grilled with sweet miso sauce), we cheat ourselves of the taste of three centuries of travel in the Kiso.

THE WALKS BETWEEN post towns along the Kiso Road are not particularly taxing: some are as short as three and a half hours, some as long as six. Most of the scenery between the towns is stunningly beautiful, and there is plenty of opportunity to empty the mind and find one's pace. There are quaint mountain villages, small towns that take you back hundreds of years, and large towns like Kiso Fukushima with historical sites well worth visiting.

For travelers specifically interested in the history and culture of the Kiso or the Edo-period walking culture of Japan, there are a number of books that might be read beforehand, some of which are noted in the "Suggested Reading" section at the end of this book. And, although most Japanese (particularly younger ones) can understand simple English when it's spoken slowly and clearly, a short Japanese phrase book may come in handy.

But for traveling the Kiso Road, you really need very little: a few material essentials, an open mind, good cheer, and the determination to keep putting one foot in front of the other.

Itte irasshai!

> And what you thought you came for
> Is only a shell, a husk of meaning
> From which the purpose breaks only when it is fulfilled
> If at all.

—T. S. Eliot, *Four Quartets*, "Little Gidding"

Notes

PREFACE

1. Anciently, Kiso was written either 岐蘇, 吉蘇, or 岐曾, but today is written 木曽, meaning "an abundance of trees."

2. The Kiso Mountains average about 8,500 feet above sea level and are considered a part of the Japanese Central Alps. The tallest mountain in this range is Mount Kisokomagatake, which rises 9,698 feet above sea level. Another famous peak, visible from the post town of Magome, is Mount Ena, at 7,188 feet.

3. Road: 路. In this case a place where the traveler walks 足 and calls down the gods and spirits 各 to accompany him or her. It is interesting that the other major highways in Japan were called *do* 道, the ordinary word for road or highway. To my limited knowledge, only the Kisoji retains the more mysterious term 路.

INTRODUCTION

1. In this case, Confucius uses the word 道—a road, way, or the Way. The character indicates an intelligent way of moving forward, and ninety-nine out of a hundred translators will choose "the Way" in this passage. I prefer not to, in deference to my own context. Confucius, who was a great walker, would, I think, have approved.

CHAPTER FIVE

1. A play on words: "pine" and "wait" are both pronounced *matsu*.

2. *Goreizan:* a traditional Chinese medicine composed of five ingredients and used as a cure for fever, dry throat, and urinary problems. Even today, it is used against edema, nephritis, and hangovers.

CHAPTER SIX

1. *Minebari:* a kind of alder (*Alnus firma*).

227

Glossary

Batto Kannon: This aspect of Kannon—depicted with a horse's head on the headdress, or simply a horse's head on a human body—is believed to expel evil spirits and to protect animals, particularly horses and cattle. Stone monuments engraved with his image are found by the roadside, particularly in northern and central Japan. Iconographically, he may appear with numerous heads and with as many as eight arms. See also *Kannon*.

bodaiji: A family temple.

chaya: A teahouse, or rest house, often at the side of a road. See also *mine no chaya* and *naka no chaya*.

ch'i: The primal energy from which the world is made.

chikuwa: A kind of fish paste often hardened into a small tube.

daikon: The large white Japanese radish.

dosojin: An old man and woman, often depicted with happy smiles, who protect travelers along their way. Their images are found engraved on stone monuments along the roads in Japan, although sometimes the monument will be engraved only with the Chinese characters 道祖神. Of ancient Taoist origin, they have been incorporated into the Shinto pantheon.

furo (o-furo): The traditional Japanese bath, often made of cedar, tile, or, in times past, cast iron (a wooden false bottom is put in to keep bathers from being scorched). Before entering, the bather soaps off, rinses thoroughly, and then soaks for as long as he or she likes, depending on who's next. Some o-furo are just big enough for one person, others for as many as six. The public baths are called *sento*.

futon: The folding mattress laid on the floor for sleeping.

gaijin: Foreigner. Short for *gaikokujin*, lit., "outside country person."

guinomi: A small cup, often ceramic, used for drinking sake or tea.

gomen kudasai: Lit., "Excuse me." Used to announce oneself at an entranceway to a house or shop.

gomen nasai: An apology (e.g., "I'm sorry.").

haori: A Japanese half coat.

Heart Sutra (Hannya haramita kyo): A short sutra said to contain the essence of Buddhism.

honjin: The post town headquarters and officially designated inn for a provincial governor, warlord, or other important person.

waki-honjin: The supplementary honjin. Designated for important people, but for those less so than of honjin status.

hoshigaki: Dried persimmons. Usually prepared, peeled, strung together, and hung from a balcony.

iaido: The art of drawing the Japanese sword; sometimes called quick-draw swordsmanship.

ishitatami: Large, rough stones laid down to pave a road.

iwana: A char; a Japanese river fish (*Salvelinus pluvius*).

izakaya: A tavern or bar, often serving traditional snacks, something like Japanese tapas.

jinja: A Shinto shrine. Not to be confused with a *tera* or *o-tera,* which is a Buddhist temple. Sometimes both occupy the same grounds.

Jizo (Sanskrit, Ksitigarbha): A Buddhist bodhisattva of compassion. He appears with a shaved head, monkish robes, and a staff at the top of which are six rings. The rings not only jingle as he walks along, warning small animals to get out from underfoot, but represent the six realms within which we all transmigrate: hell, the realm of hungry ghosts, the realm of animals, the realm of humans, the realm of the angry gods, and the realm of the gods. He is particularly regarded as the savior of children, small animals, and travelers, and his stone monuments are seen by the roadside all over Japan.

kakehashi: A suspension bridge. Some were built to cross a river, but those in the Kiso were often constructed along a cliff or high bank on the side of a river.

kamidana: A household altar or small shrine for the family gods.

kampaku: The chief advisor to the emperor.

Kannon (Sanskrit, Avalokisteshvara): The Buddhist bodhisattva—sometimes referred to as a goddess—of mercy and compassion. This bodhisattva is depicted as either male or female but is always attired in beautiful flowing robes and with an otherworldly aura. Statues of Kannon are more likely to be found in temples or in temples grounds than by the roadside. Kannon is worshipped in almost all Buddhists sects in Japan. See also *Batto Kannon*.

karo: A small brazier put on a table, often lit by paraffin.

koi: 鯉, a carp. 恋, love, passion. When written in the Japanese syllabary, こい, the meaning can be intentionally vague.

koma: Colt.

konbini: The Japanese shortened pronunciation of "convenience," meaning "convenience store."

koto: A thirteen-stringed musical instrument laid horizontally on the ground. Sometimes called a "Japanese harp."

kotsuzake: Sake served over an iwana or some other river fish in a seven- or eight-inch horizontal "cup."

kumayoke: A small bell rung to scare away bears that might be on or close to a mountain trail.

mame: Bean, also meaning "blister."

mantra: A power-laden syllable or series of syllables that manifests certain cosmic forces or aspects of the buddhas. Continuous repetition of mantras is practiced as a form of meditation in many Buddhist schools (*The Shambhala Dictionary of Buddhism and Zen*).

masugata: A small square in the middle of a post town, constructed in part to slow down an invading army.

matsuri: A traditional Japanese festival, often honoring a god, a sacred object, or an event.

mine no chaya: A tea or rest house at the peak of a mountain or pass. See also *chaya*.

minshuku: An inn or private house, usually less expensive than a ryokan, lodging and serving meals to travelers. Meals are served in a common room.

mizubune: A water trough hollowed out from a single log, looking something like a small boat.

mujo: Impermanence. That all things are impermanent is one of the basic tenets of Buddhism.

naka no chaya: A tea or rest house halfway up a mountain or pass. See also *chaya*.

natto: Fermented soybeans.

nembutsu: Repetition of the sacred name of Amida Buddha (Sanskrit, Amitabha). It can be a prayer, chant, mantra, or act of devotion.

o-harai: A religious purification ceremony to cleanse both mind and body.

o-kami-san: Proprietress of an inn or eating establishment.

onsen: A hot spring. Believed to be of curative powers, some for very specific maladies.

ri: An ancient measure of distance, 2.44 miles.

ryokan: A traditional Japanese inn, with tatami floors in the guests' rooms, futon as bedding, and meals often served privately.

shakuhachi: A five-hole bamboo flute, played vertically rather than horizontally.

shojin ryori: A vegetarian meal. Usually associated with the diet of Buddhist monks, but now served in an elegant fashion at the tea ceremony and some upper-class restaurants.

shuku: A post town.

ai-no-shuku: A small way station between post towns.

shukubo: A building in a temple compound reserved for pilgrims, travelers, and sometimes students.

takasho yakusho: A special office for inspecting the gathering and raising of hawk chicks.

tansaku: A short, stiff vertical strip of paper, used for samples of calligraphic poetry.

tanuki: Called a "raccoon dog," it is neither raccoon nor dog but looks more like the former and is about the same size. Believed to be a shape-shifter and prankster, sometimes changing themselves into beautiful women and leading people astray.

tatami: The straw matting used for the floors in traditional Japanese houses. About six feet by three feet by one and a half inches thick.

toge: A mountain pass.

tokonoma: An alcove in a Japanese house, temple, or restaurant, in which is often displayed a hanging scroll, an arrangement of flowers, and/or some other artifact.

tokkuri: A small ceramic bottle for heating or serving sake.

tokubetsu junmai: An especially refined sake.

udon: Thick, white Japanese noodles.

umeboshi: A small, pickled Japanese apricot. The Japanese apricot (*Prunus mume*) is mistakenly called a "plum."

unagi: A Japanese common eel, served grilled.

yukata: An unlined cotton garment similar to a bathrobe, worn after a bath or as an informal kimono during the hot summer months. Often of blue and white design.

zakkaya: A general dry goods or grocery store.

Bibliography and Suggested Reading

WORKS IN JAPANESE

Akizato Kakishima. *Kiso meisho zukai.* Illustrated by Houkyoo Saiton (1805). Kyoto: Rinsen shoten, 1995.

Ban Kokei. *Kinsei kijin den zoku kinsei kijin den.* Tokyo: Heibonsha, 1972.

Basho zenhokku. Yamamoto Kenkichi, ed. Tokyo: Kodansha gakujutsu bunko, 2012.

Fujioka Chikuson. *Shinanoro no haijintachi.* Nagano: Shinano mainichi shinbunsha, n.d.

Fukuda Shintaro. *Nihon hyaku meizan.* Tokyo: Shincho buncho, 1964.

Haika kijin dan-Zoku haika kijin dan. Kira Sueo, ed. Tokyo: Iwanami shoten, 2009.

Heike monogatari. Vols. 1 and 2. Takagi Ichinosuke, Ozawa Masao, Atsumi Kaoru, and Kinda Ichiharuhiko, eds. Tokyo: Iwanami shoten, 1959.

Hitono Iinari. *Dare demo arukeru nakasendo rokujukyu tsugi (chukan).* Tokyo: Bungeisha, 2006.

Hojoki/Tsurezuregusa. Nishio Minoru, ed. Tokyo: Iwanami shoten, 1957.

Imai Kingo. *Konjaku nakasendo hitori annai.* Tokyo: Nihon kotsu kaisha, 1976.

Inagaki Shinichi. *Nakasendo: Mukashi to ima.* Higashi-Osaka: Houikusha, 1998.

Kaibara Ekiken. "Azumaji no ki." In *Shin nihon koten bungaku taikei,* vol. 98. Itasaka Youko and Munemasa Isoo, eds. Tokyo: Iwanami shoten, 1991.

Kishimoto Yutaka. *Nakasendo 69 tsugi wo aruku.* Nagano-shi: Shinano mainichi shinbunsha, 2001.

235

Kiso. Kiso Kyoikukai Kyodo Kanbu, ed. Nagano-shi: Shinano kyoikukai shuppanbu, 1998.

Kiso no ontakesan. Sugawara Hisakiyo et al., eds. Tokyo: Iwada Shoin, 2009.

Kisomura monogatari. Okubo Miyama and Yukawa Takeo, ed. Yabuhara: Kisomura kominkan, 1982.

Kitamura Enkin. *Tsukiyama teizoden* (1735). Tokyo: Kashima shoten, 1989.

Nakasendo wo aruku. Yama to Keikokusha Osaska Shikyoku, ed. Tokyo: Yama-kei, 2000.

Nomura Shigeo. *Roshi/soshi.* Tokyo: Kadokawa bunkyo, 2004.

Okada Zenkuro. *Kisojun koki.* Wakita Masahiko, ed. Ichinomiya-shi: Ichinomiya shidan kai, 1973.

Takahashi Chihaya. *Edo no tabibito: Daimyo kara toubousha made 30 nin no tabi.* Tokyo: Shueisha, 2005.

Takuan osho zenshu. Vol. 3. Takuan Osho Zenshu Kankokai, ed. Tokyo: Kogeisha, 1929.

Yasumi Roan. *Ryoko yojin shu.* (1810). Sakurai Masanobu, trans. to modern Japanese. Tokyo: Yasaka shobo, 2009

WORKS IN ENGLISH

Dotzenko, Grisha F. *Enku: Master Carver.* Tokyo: Kodansha International, 1976.

Eliot, T. S. *Collected Poems, 1909–1962.* London: Faber and Faber, 1963.

Hori Ichiro. *Folk Religion in Japan.* Chicago: University of Chicago Press, 1968.

Kaibara Ekiken. *Cultivating Ch'i* (*Yojokun*). Translated by William Scott Wilson. Boston: Shambhala, 2008.

Morse, Edward S. *Japanese Homes and Their Surroundings.* Mineola, NY: Dover Publications, 1961.

Nenzi, Laura. *Excursions in Identity.* Honolulu: University of Hawaii Press, 2008.

Tanahashi, Kazuaki. *Enku: Sculptor of a Thousand Buddhas.* Boulder, CO: Shambhala, 1982.

Tschumi, Christian. *Mirei Shigemori: Modernizing the Japanese Garden.* Berkeley, CA: Stone Bridge Press, 2005.

Vaporis, Constantine Nomikos. *Breaking Barriers*. Cambridge, MA: Harvard University Press, 1994.

Weston, Walter. *The Playground of the Far East*. London: John Murray, 1918.

White, Merry. *Coffee Life in Japan*. Berkeley, CA: University of California Press, 2012.

SUGGESTED READING

Blacker, Carmen. *The Catalpa Bow*. London: George Allen & Unwin, 1975.

Gil, Robin D. *Topsy-Turvy 1585*. Key Biscayne, FL: Paraverse Press, 2005.

Ikku Jippensha. *Shank's Mare (Hizakurige)*. Translated by Thomas Satchell. Rutland, VT: Tuttle, 1960.

Martin, Samuel E. *Essential Japanese*. Tokyo: Tuttle, 1954.

Nenzi, Laura. *Excursions in Identity*. Honolulu: University of Hawaii Press, 2008.

Statler, Oliver. *Japanese Inn*. New York: Random House, 1961.

The Tale of the Heike (Heike monogatari). Translated by Hiroshi Kitagawa and Bruce T. Tsuchida. Tokyo: University of Tokyo Press, 1975.

The Vintage Book of Walking. Duncan Minshull, ed. London: Vintage, 2000.

Toson, Shimazaki. *Before the Dawn*. Translated by William E. Naff. Honolulu: University of Hawaii Press, 1987.

Tuan, Yi-Fu. *Topophilia*. New York: Columbia University Press, 1974.

Weston, Walter. *Mountaineering and the Exploration of the Japanese Alps*. London: John Murray, 1896.

Weston, Walter. *The Playground of the Far East*. London: John Murray, 1918.

Books and Translations
by William Scott Wilson

The 36 Strategies of the Martial Arts: The Classic Chinese Guide for Success in War, Business, and Life, by Hiroshi Moriya

The Book of Five Rings, by Miyamoto Musashi

Cultivating Ch'i: A Samurai Physician's Teachings on the Way of Health, by Kaibara Ekiken

The Demon's Sermon on the Martial Arts: And Other Tales, by Issai Chozanshi

Hagakure: The Book of the Samurai, by Yamamoto Tsunetomo

The Life-Giving Sword: Secret Teachings from the House of the Shogun, by Yagyu Munenori

The Lone Samurai: The Life of Miyamoto Musashi

Master of the Three Ways: Reflections of a Chinese Sage on Living a Satisfying Life, by Hung Ying-ming

The One Taste of Truth: Zen and the Art of Drinking Tea

The Pocket Samurai

The Spirit of Noh: A New Translation of the Classic Noh Treatise the Fushikaden, by Zeami

The Swordsman's Handbook: Samurai Teachings on the Path of the Sword

Tao Te Ching: A New Translation, by Lao Tzu

The Unfettered Mind: Writings from a Zen Master to a Master Swordsman, by Takuan Sōhō